Prayers
for Prisoners

Prayers for Prisoners

Ann Ball
and Maximilian, S.F.O.

Our Sunday Visitor Publishing Division
Our Sunday Visitor, Inc.
Huntington, Indiana 46750

Nihil Obstat:
Rev. Msgr. James B. Anderson, S.T.D.
Imprimatur:
Most Reverend Joseph A. Fiorenza, D.D.
Bishop of Galveston-Houston
January 16, 2002

The *Nihil Obstat* and *Imprimatur* are official declarations that a book or pamphlet is free from doctrinal or moral error. It is not implied that those who have granted the *Nihil Obstat* and *Imprimatur* agree with the contents, opinions, or statements expressed.

Our Sunday Visitor Publishing Division
Our Sunday Visitor, Inc.
200 Noll Plaza
Huntington, IN 46750

ISBN: 1-931709-00-9 (Inventory No. T4)
LCCCN: 2001135263

Cover design by Tyler Ottinger
Cover art by Esteban Escobar Hernandez
Interior design by Sherri L. Hoffman

PRINTED IN THE UNITED STATES OF AMERICA

This book is dedicated to my father and mother; may they rest in peace. To my fellow prisoners everywhere, and to all the victims of crime.

— MAX, S.F.O.

Contents

Acknowledgments

We would like to thank all those without whose prayers, encouragement, and contributions this book could not have been written. In particular, we thank Bishop Robert J. Baker of Charleston, South Carolina, for his enthusiasm for our project, and for his permission to use his lovely Litany of Our Lady of Hope. We thank our artists — Arnold Alaniz, Esteban Escobar Hernandez, Roy Martinez, Gil Lindsey, and Raul Quinteros — for the drawings that enliven these pages. Thanks, too, for the contributions from Deacon Dan Gilbert's youth group. Thanks to Father Dennis Evenson for his wonderful presentation on Our Lady of Guadalupe. To Delia "Wyatt Earp" Hernandez, our gratitude for her constant and loving support. And a very, very special thanks to Jackie Lindsey, George Foster, Tyler Ottinger, Sherri Hoffman, and all the professionals at Our Sunday Visitor for getting the book out. May it bring hope to prisoners across the United States.

Ann Ball
Max, S.F.O.

Preface

This book, *Prayers for Prisoners,* should be welcomed by many people, inside and outside prison walls.

In some way, all of us are prisoners, locked in prisons of our own or other people's making. We may be shackled by fears, addictions, negative attitudes, hostilities stemming from past experiences, inordinate attachments to people or material possessions, obsessions, bad habits, long-standing attractions to one or another form of evil, or just plain sin in general.

We may not have landed in jail for our mistakes, but without the grace of God we could have.

Though these meditations and prayers are directed mainly to prison inmates, they have a universal appeal, like the Prayer of the Lonely: "O Christ, my Savior, how is it that even though I'm surrounded by others, I still feel lonely? Is it because I have no family here, no true friends to speak of, that I feel this way?" Or the Prayer for Mercy: "Lord Jesus, in desperation I am praying and crying out to you for mercy. I am a social outcast. I have been rejected by friends and family. This is something you suffered as well.

How can I, who have been without mercy — I, a merciless one — ask for mercy? . . . I have nowhere else to turn but to you, Lord Jesus. Hear me, despite my past. Amen."

As one who formerly ministered to Catholic inmates on Florida's death row, and who regularly visited prisons and prison cells, I personally welcome this book. I wish I could have handed it to people that I visited in the past. I look forward to giving it to people in prisons I will visit or write to in the future, people I have come to call friends.

A prison can be like a monastery, for those incarcerated who desire to be people of faith. Because people in prisons have time on their hands, they can take one of two attitudes: they can make use of this forced time of incarceration as a time for spiritual growth and regeneration, or as a time for spiritual regression.

Prison life is a hard life, but it need not be a life of human and spiritual dissipation or destruction. Even life on death row can be an opportunity for growth.

Most prison inmates will see the light of day in the world outside the prison at some time in the future.

May these reflections, meditations, and prayers assist you on your spiritual journey to a world of light, rather than darkness; hope, rather than despair. I pray that the God of light and hope will be with all who make use of this book, to bring them freedom and inner peace, as only the Lord our God can; and that the Mother of God — our Lady of Ransom, of Mercy, and of Hope — will lead those who come to her in prayer closer to her Son, Jesus, who personally had the experience of being imprisoned and unjustly condemned to death. How much our Lord and God can identify with the people who have shared their faith in the meditations and prayers of this book!

Most Reverend Robert J. Baker
Bishop of Charleston
August 15, 2001
Feast of the Assumption of
the Blessed Virgin Mary

Foreword

After more than twenty years of working with "at-risk" youth, the most common thread that I have found among them is that they do not know God. They may know *of* God, but they do not know him. That is why I am so excited about this book, *Prayers for Prisoners*.

Many of the young prisoners to whom I minister do not know of the love that a connection with the Lord can bring them. That is what keeps me doing what I do. It is what keeps me going in and out of the juvenile facilities, knowing that I can help bring the message of Christ and his amazing grace to them.

The more I visit, counsel, and pray with these young people, the more Jesus' words in Matthew's Gospel come alive. He said, "I was . . . in prison and you visited me" (Mt 25:35-36).

Those words particularly came alive one day when I was talking to a thirteen-year-old boy and told him that he was a "good kid." He was surprised and responded to me, saying, "You mean after all I have done, I am still good? Jesus still loves me?" He told me that all his life everyone had told him he was no good, and that no one had ever told him that he was good.

For a long time, Jesus' words "I was in prison and you visited me" and "Whatever you did for one of these least brothers of mine, you did for me" were just words to me. But when I look into the eyes of these young ten-to-seventeen-year-olds, I do see Jesus' face. I see a Jesus who has been abandoned behind these sometimes cold and impersonal detention walls.

Although I see a confused, lost, and hurting young Jesus, I also see in their faces a searching, hopeful, and willing Jesus. In their hearts, they know that there is something missing in their lives, but they just don't know what it is. You can see them brighten up when they begin to under-stand that what they have been searching for all this time is not drugs, alcohol, sex, or money, but power. Then when they come to realize that the only power that will give them true happiness is the Power of Jesus Christ, they get very excited.

If they knew of Jesus, they did not see him as a Powerful Friend who would stick with them through it all. Instead, they saw him as a distant God who watched over them, waiting for them to do something wrong so that he could rain down pain and punishment upon them. As they come to understand that Jesus is right there, locked up with them, going through it with them, then they begin to want him even more. They come to realize that they can reach out to Jesus through prayer.

Of course, the most common prayer request that I get from these young people goes something like this: "Deacon, will you pray for me so that God will tell the judge to let me go home?"

My immediate response is "No." That usually stuns them, and you can see the look of confusion on their faces. Then I explain to them that I don't know what is best for them. I don't know that going home is the best thing for them, or that being locked up is. I can't see what is going to happen in the next minute; only God knows what is best. Only God knows what is going to happen in the next minute, day, or millennium.

I explain to them that God is not a puppet that we command to do our every wish, but a loving God who only wants what is best for us, his children. In the Lord's Prayer, we say, "Thy will be done" — and that is how I teach them to pray. It is not a prayer of "Give me this" or "Give me that." Rather, it is a prayer for God's will to be done in our lives, so that no matter what happens, we will have the comfort of knowing that it is God's will, done through his love, and that we will be all the better for it.

God has no desire for any of us to be in pain or to suffer. Since the beginning of time, he has sent us help to try to get us out of our pain that we have created, pain that we have gotten ourselves into through our falling to temptation. His goal is to have us one with him and not separate from him. We conveniently blame God for not doing his part, when it is we who are not doing our part. God has given us all that we need to succeed. He has given us all that we need to live a life of true happiness.

"Happiness" can be a funny word, though. We think of being happy as a time when there is nothing wrong and no suffering in our lives. As Christians, we have to learn the real understanding of happiness. It does not mean that we will not suffer, or that everything is always perfect in our lives. It means that as Christians, even though we go through pain and suffering, we know that God will get us through it. We have hope, knowing that whatever we are going through in our lives, Our Lord has gone through it already. Jesus knows the way out of the pain. All we have to do is come to him in prayer, seeking out the right direction. He knows the way — for, as he told us, he is the Way, the Truth, and the Life.

Jesus, who is also the Light of the world, will light the way for us with his truth. When these young people come to realize Jesus' truth, then they come to understand that the trick of the enemy is to cause us to think that who we are is based on the kind of car we drive, or the shoes we wear, or how big the bankroll in our pocket is. By drawing closer to God, they come to realize that the message the world gives us — "I have to be on top" — is *not* the message of the Gospel. The message of the Gospel is: "The last will be first, and the first will be last" (Mt 20:16).

That is a hard pill to swallow, when all we see on TV or in the movies or hear on the radio is that you have to step on and over everyone to get to the top. I help them to understand that when we get to the top without Jesus, we also fall to the bottom without him. But when we rise to the top with Jesus, we rise on a foundation that will not fall. It is an everlasting foundation that will allow Jesus' light to shine from him to us, and we will glow forever.

The Bible tells us that Jesus grew in wisdom. That is how it is for all of us. We all grow in wisdom as we come closer to God. Prayer draws us closer to him, for every time we call his name, we get his attention and he answers. We just have to call upon him, and he is right there.

Two thousand years ago, Jesus was arrested, imprisoned, tried, convicted, and executed. Two thousand years later, the same thing happens. Every time one of these young juveniles is arrested or convicted, so is Jesus. For they are the least of his people, and whatever is done to them or for them is done to Jesus. After the Crucifixion, though, came the Resurrection — and Jesus rose and was glorified.

The same thing happens to the young Jesuses that are incarcerated. If they go through this crucifixion *with* him, they will rise *with* him. My prayer is that all those who are imprisoned in juvenile facilities, in adult correctional facilities, or imprisoned in the heart will use the prayers of this book to help them resurrect their lives and bring Christ out of prison. May God the Father bless all who read it. May the peace of Christ comfort all who use the prayers here. And may the Holy Spirit help all who put these prayers into their heart to replace the chains of imprisonment with the Crown of Glory that Jesus has for all of us.

DEACON DAN GILBERT
Diocese of Galveston-Houston

INTRODUCTION I:
The Voice of Conversion

I write this with reluctance because I'm certain that there are many others, behind bars and in the free world, whose conversion stories are more interesting and spiritual. But maybe I'm supposed to write this because God often uses the ordinary, simple things to manifest himself, his Son, Jesus, and the Holy Spirit in one's life.

I was baptized and raised as a Catholic, but I was never too eager to attend Mass. God must have a great sense of humor, because at one point in my young life we moved to a neighborhood where the church was only a half block from our front door. Need I mention that my mom would still have to escort me there?

I don't recall attending church often as a teenager. I guess the turmoil of the 1960s filtered down to me. Shortly after reaching my seventeenth birthday, I joined the Army. My attendance at chapel call was almost nil — although I do remember an occasion or two of "foxhole faith," but it didn't last.

After getting out of the Army, I came back home and settled into everyday life. I eventually married, had a son, and, sadly, divorced shortly thereafter. Then began a period in my life of many relationships, increased use of alcohol and pills, and much uncertainty. God was the furthest thing from my mind and heart.

I thought I was doing okay because I eventually found a great-paying job, met the most wonderful woman, bought a brand-new home, and was making plans for marriage. I didn't need God, I thought, but I knew something was missing. I often wonder how many Rosaries my mom offered up on my behalf.

I was working as a lineman for a major electric company. I traveled quite a bit and stayed out of town frequently. After work hours, my time was mostly spent drinking.

Once, I remember being in a motel room asleep. It must have been around one o'clock in the morning. I sat straight up in bed. What had awakened me was a clear, audible voice, although I don't recall if it was male or female. It was soft, like a whisper. The voice said, "You are killing yourself." Imagine what I was thinking as I heard this! I eventually drifted off to sleep, but the voice would not be forgotten.

Not too long after, I remember thinking about all that I had in life: an upcoming marriage, a new house, good job, and money. But I thought to myself that there had to be more to life. Still, my heart and my soul were empty and bleak. Darkness was dwelling in me, and its fuel was alcohol and pills.

That darkness manifested itself one tragic night. In the process of my feeding into this darkness, a life was sadly and unnecessarily taken. All my plans and all that I thought I had earned by my own efforts were gone. Gone in the time it takes to pull a trigger.

I was arrested that night and processed into the legal system. My life had come down to this: I was placed in a cell by myself, wearing a paper gown, and placed under suicide watch. This was what my life without God had gotten me.

I was released on bond before my trial, and through the efforts and prayers of my youngest sister I came to a little place called Milagros de Cristo. I had heard of Brother Robert Morales because the Lord Jesus had used him to bring my sister to Christ. His story itself is nothing short of a miracle. Like me, he had worked for an electric company. A near-fatal accident returned him to Christ, and to a mission to bring others home.

We talked awhile, and then he took me to the chapel next door. I knelt down and Brother Robert, his mom, and my sister began to pray. I don't know how long they prayed, but suddenly I felt my right hand being raised. It was as if I were being lifted up. My eyes were closed. I saw a bright light and felt a peace and joy I had never experienced.

When I opened my eyes, we were all crying. I knew that my life would never be the same. I began to pray every day, saying the Rosary and reading the Bible, and I started to help Brother Robert in his ministry.

In time, I was sentenced to prison for my crime. When I arrived at the Michael Unit, I met the chaplain, a great guy who convinced me to join the choir. I began to write songs and sing them at the Catholic services. If some people had told me that I'd be singing songs for Christ in prison, well, I would have called them nuts.

A few years later, I was transferred to the Ellis Unit. God was blessing me tremendously. When I walked into that chapel, I knew he had sent me there. The chaplain was Richard Lopez, a humble, loving man who has the Spirit of Christ in him. He was serving Christ by being a servant to all the men in prison there.

That same year, 1994, through the efforts of the chaplain's clerk, a move was on to form a Secular Franciscan group. Some of the men were asked if they were interested, and a number of us readily said yes. A fraternity group from Houston came and guided us in our formation. Father Stephen Walsh, O.F.M., became our spiritual guide and continues to act in that capacity. Fourteen men were professed on October 28, 1995, as Secular Franciscans, and the St. Stephen/St. James Fraternity was formed. It was one of the first such groups to be professed behind prison walls. Along with the others, I embraced the Franciscan lifestyle.

It would be nice to say that all has been roses since my conversion, but it wouldn't be true. I have had my valleys and mountains. Life still goes on while one is in prison. My mom and dad both passed away within a year of each other. It was God's grace and the faith he placed in my heart and soul that sustained me then. It may sound strange, but I had to come to prison to be set free. I have my struggles, my temptations, and the days when I don't feel very Catholic or Franciscan, but I also have my Lord Jesus and my Blessed Mother to get me through those times.

I'm truly sorry for the circumstances that led me to be in here. Still, we don't know God's ways. We can only simply try to understand and seek his will for us.

I don't know when I will be released, but that's not really important. What is important is that I continue in this journey that God has sent me on. I only pray that he use me as an instrument of peace, both in this place and the world outside. And as I walk this journey, I remember a Scripture passage that my sister said was for me: "While from behind, a voice shall sound in your ears: 'This is the way; walk in it,' when you would turn to the right or to the left" (Is 30:21). May this voice speak to you as well.

MAX, S.F.O.

INTRODUCTION II:
Visiting Max

Recently, I visited Max at one of Texas' prisons for major offenders.

I hadn't visited such a prison since I was in the seventh grade and our class went on a field trip to "The Walls" in Huntsville. (I think the theory was that if we saw it, we would be less inclined to get into trouble. We were a rowdy bunch.)

Max is serving time for a crime he committed. He'll be out one day, but he will live with what he did for the rest of his life. Instead of falling into despair, he has used his time in prison to prepare for what he will do, in reparation, when he is out. He is already free because he has accepted his guilt and realized that God has forgiven him, and also importantly, he has learned to forgive himself. We hope that the prayers he has written in this book will help other prisoners find what Max has found — the very personal love of God for each of his children.

I have enjoyed collaborating with Max on this book. In his humility, he has chosen to use his Franciscan name — which, in its fullness, is Maximilian — rather than his real name, which is not printed in the book in order to spare the family of his victim any reminders. Besides, he says, "this is more God's work than mine."

The Bible tells us that we are blessed when we visit a prisoner. It doesn't, however, give us all the practical guidelines needed for a visit to a modern prison. The Bible doesn't say a thing about Ziploc bags!

The entrance to Max's prison leads from the main road through acres and acres of green, waving fields of grain. From the gate, you drive through the fields and eventually come to a stop sign. You are directed to pull over, and smiling guards ask you to raise your hood and your trunk before signing you in. The inspectors are quite helpful and answer questions for you before pointing the way to the unit you are visiting. But it would be easier if you knew what to expect in advance.

The outside is a bit intimidating, what with all the high fences, razor wire, and armed guards in their little houses high in the air. Signs mark the path to the visitors' entrance.

Max had told me I could buy him a diet Dr. Pepper, but I was instructed to leave my purse in the car. No one had told me to bring a Ziploc bag to carry things in. So I packed my pockets with some quarters, my keys, and not much else. I should have carried a hankie.

After being checked through the metal detector, I followed the sign for "Visitations" and found myself in a small room with a jailer and a computer, two pop machines, a snack machine, and a *loooong* line. Everyone but me seemed to be carrying a Ziploc bag, and some were already filled with pop and snacks, as well as quarters and keys.

The computer was "down," so I got to be in line quite a while — about an hour — and when I was finally cleared by the old method (carbon paper, no less) and got a seat, there was still a long wait while they located and "called out" Max.

One door led to the "Contact Visit Area," an outside area with picnic tables and 102-degree sunshine. The cute little jailer at the malfunctioning computer was kept hopping like the Energizer Bunny on crack because anyone who went in or out of that door had to wait until she got her eight-inch-diameter key ring and opened and relocked it with an archaic four-inch-long key.

I was sitting in front of half-inch-thick glass, which was embedded with wire mesh, when Max walked up (on the other side, naturally). The look on his face indicated how delighted he was — but he probably would have had the same look if Godzilla were visiting him. At that minute, it struck me forcefully how important visitors are to prisoners.

We had a good visit, in spite of the initial hassle of getting in, that lasted through lunchtime as we drank our diet sodas. He swore I saved him from a fate worse than death — pork chops for lunch. I told him not to dare make me cry because I had left my hankie in the car. He gave me a message for his sister and a friend; I told him to get to work on the book we were writing.

Then I just walked out to freedom, and he walked back into jail. When I left, my car was searched again, but they didn't find the memories I was taking away with me. I came home, called Max's sister to deliver his messages, and thought.

I have written to Max for over a year. But that one visit convinced me that writing wasn't enough. I could have written Max ten letters in the same amount of time it took to visit him, but then I would never have seen that look on his face or realized just how important that visit was.

I thought about something my friend Father Richard Thomas, S.J., had told me. He said one day he was reading the Bible and realized that God had told him to feed the poor, but that he never had actually, literally, done that. So one day he set out to literally feed a poor person. He took food for a hundred, and fed three hundred! He has been feeding the poor ever since.

The Bible tells us:

> "When the Son of Man comes in his glory, and all the angels with him, he will sit upon his glorious throne, and all the nations will be assembled before him. And he will separate them one from another, as a shepherd separates the sheep from the goats. He will place the sheep on his right and the goats on his left. Then the king will say to those on his right, 'Come, you who are blessed by my Father. Inherit the kingdom prepared for you from the foundation of the world. For I was hungry and you gave me food, I was thirsty and you give me drink, a stranger and you welcomed me, naked and you clothed me, ill and you cared for me, in prison and you visited me.' Then the righteous will answer him and say, 'Lord, when did we see you hungry and feed you, or thirsty and give you drink? When did we see you a stranger and welcome you, or naked and clothe you? When did we see you ill or in prison, and visit you?' And the king will say to them in reply, 'Amen, I say to you, whatever you did for one of these least brothers of mine, you did for me.' " (Mt 25:31-40)

My friend Deacon Dan Gilbert knows first-hand about prison visits. Every week he visits with the incarcerated youths in our city. Accompanied by volunteers, he brings love, the very touch of Christ, to these young people. I've been there and seen it — I've seen the love of Dan and the volunteers hit these young men and rebound back with a great swell of love in return. For some of these kids, I expect that this is their first experience of love, the kind of constant, nonjudgmental love that God is willing to give us all.

It is my hope that for all the chaplains, deacons, and laypeople involved in prison ministries, and all who visit prisoners, this little book will help in your bringing love into our prisons. And for those of us who are imprisoned in our own sins rather than physical jails, may the love of God set us free.

As for me, I think I should read my Bible a little more. Who knows what else God may be trying to say to me? And I will remember to take a Ziploc bag the next time I visit Max.

ANN BALL

I.
PRAYERS OF A PRISONER

1. Prayer for Victims

Loving Jesus, I pray that you will accept this prayer. Only through your forgiveness do I have the right to make it. I pray for all victims of crime, especially for my victims. Through acts of violence, hatred, greed, selfishness, lust, envy, and indifference I have afflicted innocent people. Through my inhumane actions, I have taken away life. I have taken away peace and joy from my victims; I have taken away the harmony and balance of everyday living. So I pray, Jesus, with all my heart and soul, restore to my victims all that I have taken. I know that a life cannot be replaced, but the ability of the victims and their loved ones to live in peace can. I pray that someday my victims will forgive me. But if they don't, please, Jesus, be merciful to them and forgive them. May all my victims have the peace that only you can give, both in this world and the next. Amen.

2. Prayer for Families

Lord Jesus and our Blessed Mother, I pray for my family and the families of all who are in prison. Bless my parents, grandparents, brothers, sisters, and children. While I am in this place, hear the prayers they offer for me and others.

Lift their spirits when they become discouraged or suffer despair. Strengthen them when the days turn into weeks, the weeks into months, and the months into years. Grant them the courage to endure when news reaches them that I didn't make parole. Sustain them with good health and blessings. If I need to be reconciled and forgive anyone in my family, humble me to do so. Lord, I pray for those in my family who don't have you in their hearts, that they open up to you. Finally, I pray that when I come home, my family and I will give you all praise and glory. Amen.

3. Prayer for Mothers

Dearest Blessed Mother, my heart cannot begin to imagine the suffering that tore through your heart and soul. Looking up at your beloved Son, what thoughts crossed your mind? Was there doubt, was there confusion, and perhaps even anger? O Blessed Virgin, now enthroned in heaven, look down on the hearts of the mothers with sons and daughters in prison. Pray for them that they may find comfort and peace. Wrap them in the mantle of your love. Wash away their doubt, confusion, and anger. Do this by your blessed tears that you shed at the foot of the cross. Amen.

4. Prayer for Those Traveling to Visit Prisoners

Jesus, beloved Savior, and Mary, our Blessed Mother, I offer this prayer for those who are traveling to visit loved ones in prison. Send your angels, Lord, to protect them on their journey. If they must travel a long distance, may the time pass quickly and safely for them. Blessed Mother, wrap them in the mantle of your love and protection. When they arrive, bless the time they visit. And when the visit is over, guide them safely home. Amen.

5. Prayer for Reconciliation

My God, my good shepherd Jesus, Blessed Mother Mary, please help me and answer my request. I need to be reconciled with (name). Through false pride, anger, ego, and unforgivingness, I have held hard thoughts about this person in my heart. I have been blinded by the darkness of hate. Please help me to make an effort to reconcile with this person. Tear down the wall of selfishness and pride that prevents me from seeking peace. If I can't see this person face-to-face, Lord, then through your Holy Spirit may I reconcile with him/her. Open my lips that I might pray for him/her. Let me see him/

her with eyes of love. Humble me, my Lord, for in my weakness, I'll be strong in you. Amen.

6. Prayer Against Temptation

Lord Jesus, help me in my struggle against temptation. Blessed Savior, you, too, were tempted by things that were pleasing to all your senses. I struggle hard against the temptation of the flesh. It comes in many forms: lust, greed, false pride, and the temptation to seek my own will. Help me, Lord Jesus, to know that there is a way out and victory over these things. When you are with me, I won't fall. It is a daily struggle, Lord Jesus, so please help me from the rising of the sun to its setting. Blessed St. Michael, be with me in this battle and help me to win over my temptations. Amen. (See page 85 for the Prayer to St. Michael.)

7. Prayer for Joy

My Lord Jesus, fill me with joy. In this place, there is much darkness. It comes in the form of anger, hatred, and despair. I ask you, Lord Jesus, to help me help others by sharing joy. May I be able to enjoy the warmth of the sunshine, the beauty of blue skies, the soothing sound of the falling rain, and the feel of the wind on my face.

All these are your gifts, and I can still enjoy them despite where I am. With your help, Jesus, grant me a joyful spirit that reflects your love and grace. Amen.

8. Prayer of the Lonely

O Christ, my Savior, how is it that even though I'm surrounded by others, I still feel lonely? Is it because I have no family here, no true friends to speak of, that I feel this way? There are people, noises, and activity. Yet, it is as if there is complete silence. Then I think of you, my Lord, hanging on your cross. Below is your mother, our Most Blessed Mother, and a few followers. Their tears and anguish are among the sounds you hear. You, my Lord, also hear the curses, taunts, and laughter. Truly, you are alone. You, the Son of God. You, God manifest in the flesh. You, the simple carpenter, the Savior of the world. As the Scriptures say, you cried out: "My God, my God, why have you forsaken me?" Lord Jesus, when I feel lonely and filled with despair, help me to realize that you felt loneliness, too. Help me to keep aware within my heart that by your living and dying, I am never alone. Amen.

9. Prayer for Mercy

Lord Jesus, in desperation I am praying and crying out to you for mercy. I am a social outcast. I have been rejected by friends and family. This is something you suffered as well. How can I, who have been without mercy — I, a merciless one — ask for mercy? As I reflect on my life filled with darkness, I can recall the many opportunities I had to exercise mercy. Yet, I didn't because I was too concerned about my needs, my wants, and no one else mattered. But now, Lord, I seek your love, which is mercy, because I don't want to be the same person I was before. Though I may not receive mercy from this system and this world, I pray that I'll receive the mercy that truly rises above all. I have nowhere else to turn but to you. Lord Jesus, hear me, despite my past. Amen.

10. Prayer for Self-forgiveness

Jesus, my Savior, I need your help. I've found that I'm able to forgive others, yet I can't forgive myself. I am overwhelmed with guilt and a sense of ego that leads me to believe I can't be forgiven for what I have done. Jesus, help me to realize that you hung on a cross for the forgiveness of my sins. By not accepting this forgiveness that was paid for with your life, basically I'm saying that wasn't good enough. Forgive me, Jesus, for my false pride and egocentric heart. Help me to realize that all the bad that I've done in my life is forgiven by your Sacrament of Reconciliation. May I embrace your heart filled with forgiveness and be held by your love, which will allow me to forgive myself. Amen.

11. Prayer for Parole

Father, I seek my freedom. I'm awaiting an answer from the authorities concerning my release. I don't know what the answer will be — may your will be done. If the answer is no, then give me the strength, faith, and will to accept this. If the answer is yes, then may I give you all the glory. Whatever the outcome, may I come to realize that I am already free. I'm free despite the walls and wire. I'm free because you sent your Son to die for me. By his death, I am truly free — forever. Amen.

12. Prayer for When the Answer Is No

Lord Jesus, I am hurting so much right now. I feel so many emotions because of things not turning out as I thought they would. I had hoped and prayed that I would find favor with the parole board. Instead, I have been told I won't be released yet. I'm sad, I'm resentful, I'm angry, and I'm disappointed. Lord Jesus, I prayed so hard, and I asked others to pray for me. Perhaps the time is not right. I need to realize that your will, not mine, must be done. I've tried doing my will, and it doesn't work. As the children of Israel wandered in the desert, so I, too, will continue to wander. Jesus, let me not be guided in my wandering by my own emotions but by your promises that you will be with me. Renew my faith and my hope, and strengthen my desire to love and serve you. For when you open the door, Jesus, there will be no turning back and I will truly be free. Amen.

13. Prayer of a New Prisoner

Dear Lord, I face an uncertain future as I begin my life in prison. My own will, my own actions, placed me in this place. In a sense, Lord, I have always been in prison. By seeking worldly ways, I had turned my back on your sacrifice, which promises eternal life. Yet now I seek to do your will, to follow the path you have set before me. In all that I do, preserve me from the darkness that will seek to blind me. I pray to you, Jesus, by your heart, your words, your eternal light, that my journey in prison will end with the peace that only you can give. Amen.

14. Prayer of a Murderer

O my God, how unworthy I am to implore your help. I feel myself to be the most unworthy of all the things you have created. For, dear God, I have murdered. I have not created life — I have destroyed it. In doing so, I made myself master of life and death, when in reality I was a slave to sin. In murdering, I showed no respect for life, for my victim(s), for others, for you, or for myself. I offer this prayer in hopes of reconciliation with you. I offer this prayer for my victim(s) as well as for the countless victims of war, abortion, and unjust punishments. In offering this prayer, I pray for your forgiveness, the forgiveness of my victim(s), and the forgiveness of the family (families) of my victim(s) — I pray that they all may be at peace. Lastly, I pray that through the precious blood of your Son, I may forgive myself. Amen.

15. Prayer of a Rapist

Jesus, I am a rapist. I am shunned and despised by society, both in the free world and in prison. It is what I deserve for my actions.

Through my actions, I have not only violated a woman's body, but I have also violated her dignity as a human being and as one of your creatures. Maybe I did what I did because of a deep-seated fear, or a desire for power because I had none; that doesn't excuse me. But now it is a greater power I seek. I need the power of your precious blood on the cross, the power of your love that can change anyone. I want your help and your love. I believe that one day I can embrace your holy cross, fall to my knees, and thank you for granting me peace and eternal life. Let today be that day. Amen.

16. Prayer for Sex Offenders

God, my Father, you sent your Son to save us. Part of what he did was to cast out demons. Today, some are still tormented by demons. Some demons take their form in our physical desires. These demons can be a desire for sexual gratification. Masturbation, pornography, and homosexuality are among the avenues some walk. Others in this place are rapists, pedophiles, and prostitutes. These are the ones who are easy to look down on, easy to judge, easy to condemn. I don't seek to understand why such things are done, God; I seek only to pray for them. I know that you did not create them to do such things. But somewhere along the path of life, things went contrary to your will. God, give me, and others, the compassion to grieve for them, to make intercession for them. Let me not judge, but let me remember that I, too, am a sinner, and that it is through your mercy that I am forgiven. Cast out their demons. In the name of your Son, Jesus, I ask that these people will find peace, mercy, and love — and let me be a vessel to bring these gifts to those who are afflicted. Amen.

17. Prayer of a Robber

Lord, I am among the most feared of all criminals; I am a robber. I preyed on people's fear and defenselessness. Rather than work for a living, I chose to take what other people worked for. At times, I did it for drugs, because I didn't want to work, or because I got a thrill from doing it. Not only did I rob my victims of their possessions, but I also robbed them of the peace and security that are every person's right. O Jesus, I am so ashamed. I placed fear into innocent people with my words and weapons. I pray that my victims will again have peace and security of mind and heart. I pray for myself, Jesus, that I can truly change and not take from people but instead give back positive things. May my hands be used for honest gain and labor through your help. Amen.

18. Prayer of a Thief

My Lord Jesus, so long ago you hung on a cross. Also hanging on a cross was a thief named Dismas. He believed in you, and you promised him paradise. At this moment, Lord, I kneel at the foot of your cross because I, too, am a thief. Lord, I have stolen from others what they had earned from their honest labor. I chose to take the wide path of the world, rather than the narrow path to you. Jesus, not only have I stolen material goods, but I've also taken what can't be bought and sold. I've stolen time by wasting it. I've stolen the talents you've given me by not using them. I've stolen the truth by lying. I've stolen courage by being fearful. I've stolen happiness by preferring sadness. Lastly, I've stolen love by being hateful, bitter, envious, and jealous. Thus, my Jesus, I plead at the foot of your cross: Please forgive me and have mercy. Jesus, I believe in you. From this moment forth, let me be filled with your spirit so that I no longer take, but only give. I ask this in your precious name. Amen.

19. Prayer of a White-collar Criminal

Lord Jesus and our Blessed Mother, I am not a violent criminal. Despite this, I am still a criminal. I have used the talents given to me by God for selfish gain. Through my own will and my deceptions, I have embezzled, swindled, cheated, and misappropriated from those who trusted me. I took and abused their money, credit cards, insurance claims, land, and other hard-earned possessions. With false speech, false intentions, and true greed, I was a fraud. I ask you, Jesus, and you, my Blessed Mother, to show me how to pray for all those I deceived. I cannot deceive you, Lord Jesus. I can never repay all that I've taken. Maybe that's not what you want from me. Maybe you want me to change my focus away from myself in order to help others. Help me, Jesus, to use my talents for good from this day forth. Blessed Mother, guard my actions and keep my heart contrite. Amen.

20. Prayer of a Veteran in Prison

Jesus, I offer this prayer for all incarcerated veterans — both those who served in war and those who served in peace. May we who once served our country proudly come to serve you, Lord Jesus. We once fought for freedom, but now we must fight the spiritual fight for ourselves, and for our comrades, seeking spiritual freedom. My prayer is for the veterans here in prison, to become stronger in serving you; and for those who don't know you, to come to experience your love. Though we are incarcerated, we still love our country, and we ask you to bless it. Lord Jesus, we also pray for our fellow servicemen and servicewomen who fell on battlefields, who died at sea or in the air. Lord, I know you won't forget them, and may we never forget them. Amen.

21. Prayer of a Prisoner on Death Row

Lord Jesus, I am condemned to die. It is true that all humans must die, but it's different when one knows the exact date. All of my actions have led to the end of the line. It is here that I await death. What I did to get me here was such that the law says it warranted my death. I may never have given you any time or thought. I may still not believe, but my options are gone. I am beyond the mercy of mankind, but I need your mercy — I am not beyond that! I ask you, Jesus, to accept my repentance for my sins, to give me courage and faith. May my victim(s), the family (families) of my victim(s), and the executioner have peace. Grant to me as well, Jesus, your peace (see Jn 14:27), which will lead me to eternal life. Amen.

22. Prayer for the Police

Lord Jesus, some of us are resentful toward the police. Perhaps some of them seem to us as the source of our troubles. Help us to remember that it was our own actions that put us here; the police were simply doing their job. Perhaps, Lord, we resent the authority they represent. Whatever the reasons, if I choose to follow you, I must begin to pray for these men and women. Help me to let go of the past and see them in a new light. Help me to realize that you love them as you love me. Help me to realize that they have families who love them, Lord, and that many of them serve you as well. Lastly, St. Michael, patron saint of police officers, I ask you to guard and protect them as they do their job. Keep them from harm, and let my prayer assist them in their lives. Amen.

23. Prayer for Juries

Lord Jesus, unlike you I had a jury to help decide my fate. More than that, you were innocent of any wrongdoing. You, my Lord, were the spotless Lamb of God who came to take

away the sins of the world. Despite your inno-
cence, you were condemned. The system of man's
law was not offered to you. Instead, you were
convicted by the world, with its anger, sin, and
greed. The choice that my jury made concerning my punishment was determined by facts and
was deliberated and thought out. I pray for these
men and women. Theirs was not a personal ven-
detta against me; they were only acting as re-
sponsible citizens. I was once part of the system
that gives the right to trial by jury. So, Lord, I
pray for all juries, those past, those present, and
those in the future. I pray that the choices and
decisions they make might not only benefit society, but also be just ones, tempered by mercy,
for those on trial. Amen.

24. Prayer for Judges

My Jesus, I offer this prayer for all judges in
the justice system. I recall my own experience
when I stood before the judge. As I awaited my
fate, I was apprehensive, hopeless, and fearful
before such great power. Now I realize the judge
was a human being, and that his decision could
not have been easy. For some of us, it was a matter of how many years we would be sentenced;
for others, it was a matter of life and death. It

may appear that some judges are indifferent, callous, or outright cruel. Yet, it is we as defendants who by our own actions placed ourselves before the judge. Jesus, let me not blame the judge. I pray that the sentences passed down will be fair and in keeping with our legal system. Give these judges patience, understanding, and wisdom, for theirs is not an easy burden to carry. But most of all, Lord, help me to remember that you are my Judge. You look on me as no earthly judge could. You have before you all that I've done — good and bad. I don't ask for justice — I ask for mercy, a mercy that I can never earn. Jesus, you are the merciful and just Judge, and this thought gives me hope that I will inherit eternal life with you. Amen.

25. Prayer for Jailers

Lord Jesus, it is hard for me to pray for my jailers. I look at the officers here and I want to judge. For the most part, they look down on me. Because I wear this prison garb, they seem to consider me less than human. I see hatred in their eyes, contempt on their faces. I hear hostility in their voices. It is so easy to respond in the same way. Yet you, too, Lord, had guards. You were beaten and treated worse than I am. Despite their actions, you never said a word against them. You did what seems impossible — you loved even them. So I pray, Jesus, let me not just see a uniform. Let me see a human being, one you died for. Let my words for them be a prayer for peace in their lives. May I see them with your eyes, Jesus, and love them as your Sacred Heart loves them. Amen.

26. Prayer for Prison Workers

My Lord Jesus, I offer this prayer on behalf of all the prisoners and others who labor in this prison. By their labor, many tasks are completed. I offer this for the cooks and other kitchen workers who prepare the meals I eat; may you bless their hands. I offer this for the laundry workers who wash and provide the clothes I wear. I offer this for the clerks who are an important part of the everyday operation of this prison; protect and bless their talents. I offer this for the janitors and orderlies who clean this prison; may their labor be a joy to you. I offer this for the field hands who labor in the hot sun or in the cold winter; by their efforts may you be glorified. Let all of us who work make our jobs a daily offering to you, Lord. Though some of our tasks are menial, may they give us a sense of responsibility and a desire for honest labor. May all our tasks be done with you in our hearts. Amen.

27. Prayer for Wardens

The responsibility is great, my Lord, for these officials. Along with this responsibility and authority, much wisdom is needed. I am subject to these people, not only because of their positions, but because your Word tells me (see Rom 13:1-5). So let me pray for them, that the decisions and choices they make may be not only for my good, but also for the good of all concerned. I pray that these authorities would seek you in prayer, in order that all their thoughts, words, and actions may be guided by God, who is the ultimate authority. Amen.

28. Prayer for Prison Administrators

Jesus, you who so humbly submitted to authority, yet who had all authority over heaven and earth; you who gave your life for my salvation, help me. Help me, Lord Jesus, to pray for the staff of this prison. I pray that the wardens may have wisdom to use their authority with concern for all prisoners. I pray for all the security officers, not to find favor with them, but that they find you. May I realize that they are human, with lives and families; that they are not merely "uniforms." May I have the strength to respond to them in a way that pleases you, no matter the circumstance, no matter if I am right or wrong. Most especially grant me, Jesus, a willing heart to be a witness for you, so that the members of the administration who don't know you may do so some day. Hear my prayer, Jesus, so all may be at peace. Amen.

29. Prayer for Priests, Chaplains, and Volunteers

Lord Jesus, you sent your Holy Spirit to guide us. I believe that the priests, chaplains, and volunteers involved in prison ministry are sent and guided by that same Spirit. Give them all the gifts necessary in order that they may serve you, Jesus, by helping me. I pray that you give them open ears to listen, bold voices to proclaim your Word, a strong shoulder to lean on in sad times, and spiritual wisdom to counsel me. When they become weary, burdened by all the problems of their ministry, renew them, Lord, with your strength and blessings. Lastly, when I look into their eyes, may I see your love and compassion reflected there. Amen.

30. Prayer for a Chaplain

God in heaven, I beseech you to grant your blessings and grace upon Chaplain (name). Give the chaplain strength when the hours of his ministry are long. Give him the ability to understand the problems and the concerns of those who come to him for advice and comfort. Give the chaplain the desire to tell us through his homilies about you, the Father; Jesus, your Son; the Holy Spirit; and the Blessed Mother and all the saints. Give him the words of prayer to express the needs and desires of all who ask for prayer. May he find favor with the administration, in order that your will be done. May he be an example of someone who loves you and seeks to serve you. By that example, may we seek to do the same. Amen.

31. The Way of the Cross for Prisoners

(May we, as prisoners, use these prayers not only during the Lenten season but also when we are undergoing our own sufferings. Let us ponder all the stations in the following Way of the Cross for Prisoners, in the hope that we will not be the same as when we began our journey. — Max)

Lord Jesus, guided by the Holy Spirit and aided by all your angels and saints, may we who are imprisoned undertake this sorrowful journey with you. May our hearts, thoughts, and spirits embrace all that you endured for us as you suffered. When the journey is over, let us all rest in your loving embrace.

I. Jesus Is Condemned to Death

We, too, have stood before the judge. We have faced those who wanted nothing but our pain and suffering. The feeling at the moment of our sentencing was a hollowness of our souls. Still, we must pay for our transgressions; you, O Lord, were innocent.

> When I face condemnation,
> Jesus, I trust in you.
> When I face uncertainty,
> Jesus, I trust in you.

II. Jesus Carries His Cross

O my Jesus, upon your sacred shoulder you bore the cross. But it was not the heavy wood that was a burden; it was my sins. I need a renewal of my faith in order that I can bear the crosses in my life.

> When I am burdened,
> Jesus, I trust in you.

When I need faith,
Jesus, I trust in you.

III. Jesus Falls the First Time

How your enemies must have rejoiced as you fell, my Lord. Still, it was your intention to get up and suffer again. Lord, at times I, too, have the best intentions, yet I stumble and fall.

When I fail to stand for you,
Jesus, I trust in you.
When those who want me to suffer are rejoicing,
Jesus, I trust in you.

IV. Jesus Meets His Sorrowful Mother

O Lord Jesus, how your heart and your mother's heart must have ached. No words were spoken, just a reflection of love and sorrow in your faces. Help me to find the words for my family, to be a reflection of your love, to let them know you are with me and with them.

When my family aches for me,
Jesus, I trust in you.
When the sorrow of my family is heavy,
Jesus, I trust in you.

V. Simon of Cyrene Helps Jesus Carry the Cross

You, the Son of Man, are struggling with the cross, and one among the crowd gives you help. How often do my pride and ego get in the way of those who want to help me.

> When I fail to see your help,
> Jesus, I trust in you.
> That I may accept help,
> Jesus, I trust in you.

VI. Veronica Wipes the Face of Jesus

Veronica displayed courage in coming to aid you. Amid all the hatred, she showed love and compassion. She was not ashamed to serve her Lord. Grant me courage to truly serve you, most especially here inside the walls of a prison, where being a Christian is not easy.

> When I need courage,
> Jesus, I trust in you.
> When I need to show love,
> Jesus, I trust in you.

VII. Jesus Falls the Second Time

Jesus, you fall again. I fall again. I ask for renewed strength and faithfulness. I can't bear my crosses without your help.

When I grow weary,
Jesus, I trust in you.
When I am falling,
Jesus, I trust in you.

VIII. *Jesus Speaks to the Women of Jerusalem*

Your beloved followers shed tears of anguish and sorrow. Yet, you seek to comfort them. In prison, it is seen as weakness to shed tears. Give me strength to be weak for love of you and your sufferings.

When I am ashamed to cry,
Jesus, I trust in you.
When I need to cry,
Jesus, I trust in you.

IX. *Jesus Falls the Third Time*

The constant pain and suffering cause you to grow weary and fall. May I be reminded that it is my lack of repentance that causes me to fall.

When I need to repent,
Jesus, I trust in you.
When I feel like quitting,
Jesus, I trust in you.

X. Jesus Is Stripped of His Garments

Lord, those who think they have power over you take away your last possessions. So, too, when we enter prison, we are stripped of possessions. More than that, we are stripped of dignity and human quality. Let me remember that earthly possessions, earthly dignity, are not important in your eyes.

When I am stripped of all I own,
Jesus, I trust in you.
When I need to regain self-worth,
Jesus, I trust in you.

XI. Jesus Is Nailed to the Cross

Lord, I cannot even begin to imagine the pain you endured. I, too, have inflicted pain on others, those who were innocent as you were. Give me a new heart that seeks to give love, not pain.

When I think of my sins,
Jesus, I trust in you.
When I am suffering,
Jesus, I trust in you.

XII. *Jesus Dies on the Cross*

Finally, it is finished. My Lord Jesus has given up his spirit. By your death, Lord, renew my spirit and free me to serve and love you through others.

When I think of your holy cross,
Jesus, I trust in you.
When I need your spirit,
Jesus, I trust in you.

XIII. Jesus' Body Is Taken Down from the Cross

The grief is overwhelming. Your mother holds your lifeless body in her trembling arms. Help me to take you down from the cross by keeping from sin. May your Blessed Mother hold all prisoners. May I pray for my fellow prisoners as well as for my own concerns.

> When I feel helpless,
> Jesus, I trust in you.
> When I am tempted,
> Jesus, I trust in you.

XIV. Jesus' Body Is Laid in the Tomb

Your lifeless body is placed in a lonely tomb. But the grave will not hold you. Afterward, there will be joy. Help me, a prisoner, to endure my journey in this place. Then, after all the pain, tears, and loneliness are over, let me rejoice in the freedom your cross has given me.

> When I am lonely,
> Jesus, I trust in you.
> When the journey is over,
> Jesus, I trust in you.

II.
CATHOLIC PRAYERS

1. The Sign of the Cross

We make the Sign of the Cross to show our faith, both in our redemption by Christ and in the Trinity. The making of this sign has been practiced from the earliest centuries. In early times, Christians made the Sign of the Cross on their foreheads. Later, the words "In the name of the Father, and of the Son, and of the Holy Spirit" were added.

In the third century, Tertullian reported this touching and beautiful early Christian practice by writing, "In all our undertakings — when we enter a place or leave it; before we dress; before we bathe; when we take our meals; when we light the lamps in the evening; before we retire at night; when we sit down to read; before each new task — we trace the Sign of the Cross on our foreheads."

Today, we say the same words, and using the joined fingers of our right hand, we touch ourselves on the forehead, the middle of the breast, our left side, and our right side to mark the cross. We make the sign slowly and reverently.

Among Spanish-speaking people, sometimes two Signs of the Cross are used together, one following the other. The thumb and forefinger are crossed to form a cross. First, the *persignarse*, or "signing yourself," is made by making the Sign of the Cross on the forehead, the mouth, and the breast. In Spanish, the person prays a brief prayer, which translates: "By the sign of the holy cross, deliver us, Lord, from our enemies." Then the *santiguarse*, or "blessing yourself" (the regular Sign of the Cross), is made. At the conclusion, with thumb and forefinger still forming a cross, the person puts his hand to his lips and kisses the cross thus formed. This signing is done whenever a person is entering or passing by a church, and at other times such as when an ambulance or fire truck is passing, on a visit to a cemetery, and so on.

> In the name of the Father, and of the Son, and of the Holy Spirit. Amen.

2. Amen

Amen is the word we usually say at the end of our prayers. But what does it mean? The word comes from the Hebrew language and means "Truly, it is true." In the Gospels, Christ used the word to add a note of authority to his statements. In other New Testament writings, just as the Hebrews used it, the word was a final conclusion to doxologies, or praises of God. We use it today to end our prayers, to show that we agree to and accept God's will.

3. The Apostles' Creed

A creed is a brief summary of essential Christian doctrine in language officially approved by the Church. The word itself is derived from the Latin *credo*, meaning "I believe." The Apostles' Creed, the earliest and simplest statement of beliefs of the Church, is used today by Catholics, Episcopalians, Methodists, and several other denominations. Though not actually composed by the apostles, the creed probably originated in the first century.

I believe in God, the Father almighty,
    creator of heaven and earth.

I believe in Jesus Christ, his only Son, our
    Lord.
    He was conceived by the power of the
        Holy Spirit
        and born of the Virgin Mary.
    He suffered under Pontius Pilate,
        was crucified, died, and was buried.
    He descended to the dead.
    On the third day he rose again.
    He ascended into heaven,

and is seated at the right hand of the
Father.
He will come again to judge the living and
the dead.

I believe in the Holy Spirit,
the holy catholic Church,
the communion of saints,
the forgiveness of sins,
the resurrection of the body,
and the life everlasting. Amen.

4. The Lord's Prayer (Our Father)

In response to the request of his disciples to teach them how to pray, Christ gave them the prayer commonly known as the Lord's Prayer (see Mt 6:9-13). In the early Church, the prayer was learned shortly after baptism. About the year 400, catechumens, or those wishing to join the Church, were allowed to learn the prayer as part of their preparation for baptism.

Today we pray the Lord's Prayer at Mass, just before the reception of the Eucharist, and also as a private devotion.

Our Father, who art in heaven, hallowed be thy name; thy kingdom come; thy will be done on earth as it is in heaven. Give us this day our daily bread; and forgive us our trespasses as we forgive those who trespass against us; and lead us not into temptation, but deliver us from evil. Amen.

During Mass, the prayer is ended with this acclamation:

For the kingdom, the power, and the glory are yours, now and for ever.

5. The Hail Mary

This is a prayer addressed to the Blessed Virgin Mary. The prayer has three parts. First, it has the words addressed to Mary by the archangel Gabriel at the Annunciation. Next are the words that Mary's cousin Elizabeth said at the Visitation. At the end, there is a petition in which we ask Our Lady for her help always. The prayer in this form has been prayed by Catholics for over five hundred years.

Hail, Mary, full of grace, the Lord is with thee; blessed art thou among women, and blessed is the fruit of thy womb, Jesus. Holy Mary, Mother of God, pray for us sinners, now and at the hour of our death. Amen.

6. The Glory Be (The Doxology)

The Doxology, or the Glory Be, is a short formula of praise. The custom began in the Jewish synagogue before the time of Christ. The ancient Christian Doxology began in the Oriental, or Eastern, Church. The second part of the prayer was probably added during the time of Constantine. The prayer began to be used by the Western Church around the fifth century. It became very popular and spread throughout the world.

Glory be to the Father, and to the Son, and to the Holy Spirit. As it was in the beginning, is now, and ever shall be, world without end. Amen.

7. The *Memorare*

One of the most beautiful of the Marian prayers, the *Memorare*, is attributed to St. Bernard of Clairvaux. He is a founder of the Cistercian Order. One of six brilliant sons of a French nobleman, Bernard decided to join the new monastery at Cîteaux in 1113. Within two years, he was sent to establish a new house at Clairvaux. Bernard's personal fame spread quickly, despite his shy nature, and he was drawn into public affairs. In spite of his immense activity and chronic ill health, he was a prolific writer.

He is a Doctor of the Church. His love and trust in Mary is shown in this prayer.

> Remember, O most gracious Virgin Mary, that never was it known that anyone who fled to your protection, implored your help, or sought your intercession was left unaided. Inspired by this confidence, I fly unto you, O Virgin of Virgins, my Mother. To you I come, before you I stand, sinful and sorrowful. O Mother of the Word incarnate, despise not my petitions, but in your mercy hear and answer me. Amen.

8. The Rosary

The Rosary commemorates fifteen events in the life of Jesus and Mary. These are the happenings, or "mysteries," that we think about while we recite the prayers. Today, the Rosary is usually prayed on a circle of fifty-four beads joined with a medal from which hangs a pendant of five beads and a crucifix. Although there are fifteen mysteries in the entire Rosary, people generally pick one set of mysteries to use each day.

How to Pray the Rosary

1. On the crucifix, make the Sign of the Cross and say the Apostles' Creed.

2. On the first large bead, say the Our Father.

3. On each of the three small beads, say a Hail Mary.

4. Say the Glory be to the Father.

5. Announce the first mystery; then say the Our Father (on the next large bead).

6. While thinking about the first mystery, say ten Hail Marys on the first set of ten beads.

7. Say the Glory be to the Father.

8. Announce the second mystery, then say the Our Father (on the following large bead).

9. Continue around the circle of beads, announcing the mystery and saying the prayers vocally while you think about the mystery.

10. You may end the Rosary with the Hail Holy Queen, the Fátima Prayer, or any prayer you choose.

The Joyful Mysteries

1. **The Annunciation:** The archangel Gabriel comes from God to Mary and announces that she will be the mother of the Redeemer. She accepts.

2. **The Visitation:** Mary travels to visit her cousin Elizabeth, who is to be the mother of John the Baptist, and shares with her the good news from the angel.

Praying the Rosary

Second Mystery:
Our Father, etc.

Glory Be to
the Father

Hail Mary
(ten times)

First Mystery:
Our Father

Conclusion:
Hail Holy Queen
or Fátima Prayer

Glory Be to
the Father

Hail Mary
(three times)

Our Father

Sign of the Cross
and Apostles' Creed

3. **The Nativity:** After a difficult journey, Christ is born in a stable. Shepherds visit the baby.

4. **The Presentation:** Mary and Joseph take Jesus to present him in the Temple, in accordance with Jewish law. There, Simeon and Anna recognize that the Redeemer has come.

5. **The Finding in the Temple:** Jesus is lost, but after searching for three days his parents are overjoyed to find him in the Temple.

The Sorrowful Mysteries

1. **The Agony in the Garden:** In the Garden of Gethsemane, Jesus is prostrated in an agony of blood and sweat as he contemplates and accepts his Passion and impending death.

2. **The Scourging at the Pillar:** After his arrest, Jesus is stripped, tied to a post, and whipped cruelly.

3. **The Crowning with Thorns:** The soldiers put a crown of thorns on Jesus' innocent head. They spit on him and mock him, calling him the King of the Jews.

4. **The Carrying of the Cross:** Jesus is forced to carry his own cross to his crucifixion.

5. **The Crucifixion:** Jesus is nailed to a cross and raised between two thieves. After three hours of suffering, he bows his head and dies.

The Glorious Mysteries

1. **The Resurrection:** The third day after his death, Jesus rises from the tomb and appears to his friends.
2. **The Ascension:** Jesus blesses his friends on the Mount of Olives, then he raises his hands and ascends into heaven.
3. **The Descent of the Holy Spirit:** As the apostles are gathered, the Holy Spirit, in the form of tongues of fire, descends on them.
4. **The Assumption:** After Mary's life on earth ends, she is taken up, body and soul, to heaven.
5. **The Coronation of Mary as Queen of Heaven and Earth:** Mary is received into heaven by her divine Son, and in the presence of all the angels and saints she is crowned Queen of heaven and earth.

Hail Holy Queen

Hail, holy Queen, mother of mercy, our life, our sweetness, and our hope. To you do we cry, poor, banished children of Eve. To you do we send up our sighs, mourning, and weeping in this valley of tears. Turn, then, most gracious advocate, your eyes of mercy toward us, and after this our exile show unto us the blessed fruit of your womb, Jesus. O clement, O loving, O sweet Virgin Mary.

The Fátima Prayer

O my Jesus, forgive us our sins. Save us from the fires of hell. Lead all souls to heaven, especially those who are in most need of your mercy.

9. The Stations of the Cross

The Stations of the Cross are fourteen scenes that symbolize important events in the Passion and death of Our Lord. This is the most popular devotion during Lent.

The devotion originated in the Holy Land during the time of the Crusades, when knights and pilgrims began to follow the route of Christ's way to Calvary in prayerful meditation, according to the ancient practice of pilgrims. The devotion spread throughout Europe and developed into its present form through the zealous efforts of Franciscan friars in the fourteenth and fifteenth centuries.

Devotion to the Passion actually began with the Crucifixion. According to a pious tradition, the Blessed Mother walked over and over the narrow streets that led from the court of Pilate to the gate of the Holy City. From time to time along the road sanctified by Jesus' suffering and consecrated by his blood, the Sorrowful Mother knelt and prayed.

Likewise, the apostles, disciples, and friends of Jesus who lived in Jerusalem and the surrounding areas walked this hallowed way of memories, meditating anew on the sufferings of their Master and Redeemer.

Later, only a few of the faithful were actually able to make the trip to Jerusalem and walk in the footsteps of Christ on the Way of Sorrows, from the ruined court of Pilate to the basilica on the hill of Calvary. Thus, the Franciscans brought the devotion to Europe and the rest of the world by erecting replicas of the places in Jerusalem so that the people could more easily meditate on the Passion and death of Christ.

Many beautiful meditations have been written for this devotion. In this book, there are a set of stations especially for prisoners (see page 57). Many of today's meditations add a fifteenth station in honor of the Resurrection. Here are the fourteen traditional stations. The traditional refrain said at the end of each meditation is:

V. We adore you, O Christ, and we bless you.

R. **Because by your holy cross you have redeemed the world.**

  I. Jesus Is Condemned to Death

  II. Jesus Carries His Cross

   III. Jesus Falls the First Time

   IV. Jesus Meets His Sorrowful Mother

    V. Simon of Cyrene Helps Jesus Carry the Cross

   VI. Veronica Wipes the Face of Jesus

  VII. Jesus Falls the Second Time

 VIII. Jesus Speaks to the Women of Jerusalem

   IX. Jesus Falls the Third Time

    X. Jesus Is Stripped of His Garments

   XI. Jesus Is Nailed to the Cross

  XII. Jesus Dies on the Cross

 XIII. Jesus' Body Is Taken Down from the Cross

 XIV. Jesus' Body Is Laid in the Sepulcher (Tomb)

Traditionally, the meditations on the fourteen stations are somber and sad. When a fifteenth station — in honor of the Resurrection — is added, it is a joyful remembrance of the "crowning truth" of our Christian faith (see *Catechism of the Catholic Church*, no. 638).

10. The *Via Lucis* (Way of the Light)

The *Via Lucis*, or the "Way of the Light," is a new devotion with characteristics similar to the Stations of the Cross that can be prayed personally or in community. Here, instead of a cross, a symbol of the Resurrection is carried, and the meditations are on Christ's actions from the time of the Resurrection to Pentecost. The primary function of the Way of the Light is to remind the faithful to live the Easter spirituality according to 1 Corinthians 15:1-8.

Here are the fourteen suggested stations for the Way of the Light.

I. Jesus Rises from the Dead

II. The Disciples Find the Empty Tomb

III. Jesus Appears to Mary Magdalene

IV. Jesus Walks with the Disciples to Emmaus

V. Jesus Reveals Himself in the Breaking of Bread

VI. Jesus Appears to the Disciples

VII. Jesus Confers on His Disciples the Power to Forgive Sins

VIII. Jesus Confirms Thomas in Faith

IX. Jesus Appears to His Disciples on the Shore of Lake Galilee

X. Jesus Confers Primacy on Peter

XI. Jesus Entrusts His Disciples with a Universal Mission

XII. Jesus Ascends into Heaven

XIII. Mary and the Disciples Await the Holy Spirit

XIV. Jesus Sends the Spirit Promised by the Father to His Disciples

11. Act of Faith, Hope, and Charity and Act of Contrition

When one accepts a truth on the authority of God alone, he is making an act of faith, which is an act very pleasing to God. Hope is the expectation that you will be granted the means of salvation and will gain eternal happiness. This is based not on our own power but on trust in God's promises and his mercy. Love is an act of our will. We should love God with all our heart, and we should love others for his sake. Charity is another name for love. If we are sincerely sorry for our sins, we make an act of contrition.

Act of Faith, Hope, and Charity (Love)

My God, I believe in you, I trust in you, I love you above all things, with all my heart and mind and strength. I love you because you are supremely good and worth loving; and because I love you, I am sorry with all my heart for offending you. Lord, have mercy on me, a sinner. Amen.

Act of Contrition

My God, I am sorry for my sins with all my heart. In choosing to do wrong and failing to do good, I have sinned against you whom I should love above all things. I firmly intend, with your help, to do penance, to sin no more, and to avoid whatever leads me to sin. Our Savior Jesus Christ suffered and died for us. In his name, my God, have mercy. Amen.

12. Morning Offering

The Morning Offering is a prayer recited each morning, offering the day in union with Christ's self-offering. The most commonly used form in the United States is that used by the Apostleship of Prayer. This is an association that has spread worldwide to promote the glory of God and the salvation of souls through constant prayer, particularly to the Sacred Heart of Jesus. Daily, the members make an offering and pray for the intentions of the pope. You may write to the association at: Apostleship of Prayer, 3 Stephen Ave., New Hyde Park, NY 11040.

O Jesus, through the Immaculate Heart of Mary, I offer you all my prayers, works, joys, and sufferings of this day, for all the intentions of your Sacred Heart, in union with the Holy Sacrifice of the Mass throughout the world, in reparation for my sins, for the intentions of all our associates, and in particular for the intention recommended this month by the Holy Father.

13. Mealtime Prayers

The custom of saying prayers before and after meals goes back to the days of the apostles. St. Paul wrote to the Corinthians, "So whether you eat or drink, or whatever you do, do everything for the glory of God" (1 Cor 10:31). The earliest Christians followed his advice. Before meals, they blessed their food, asking God's blessing for what they were about to eat. They said grace, which means thanks, after their meals, thanking God for providing for their bodily needs.

Clement of Alexandria, who lived in the third century, wrote, "Before taking nourishment, it is fitting to praise the Creator of all things. It is proper to sing his praises when we take as food the things created by him." Tertullian, who lived in the same century, wrote, "We do not dine until we have prayed to God. In like manner, prayer ends the feast." In saying prayers before and after meals, Catholics follow the example set by our forefathers in the faith.

Blessing Before Meals

Bless us, O Lord, and these your gifts, which we are about to receive from your bounty, through Christ our Lord. Amen.

Grace After Meals

We give you thanks, almighty God, for all your benefits, who live and reign forever. And may the souls of the faithful departed, through the mercy of God, rest in peace. Amen.

14. Prayer to St. Michael

St. Michael the Archangel's leadership in the battle against the forces of evil is vividly depicted in the Book of Revelation (12:7-9). This prayer, which was composed toward the end of the nineteenth century by Pope Leo XIII, can be especially helpful when prayed during times of temptation.

St. Michael the Archangel, defend us in battle, be our defense against the wickedness and snares of the devil. May God rebuke him, we humbly pray; and do thou, O prince of the heavenly host, by the power of God, thrust into hell Satan and the other evil spirits who prowl about the world for the ruin of souls. Amen.

15. Prayer Before a Crucifix

The cross, the symbol of mankind's redemption, has been used since the early days of the Church. Today it is present in all Catholic and most Christian churches.

During the earliest days of the Church, when Christians were being persecuted, the cross was often disguised as a part of other symbols, such as an anchor. Around the year 326, St. Helena searched for and found the true cross. Years earlier, her son Constantine the Great made a remarkable impact on the history of the world by ending the Roman Empire's persecution of Christians. In 312, while preparing for a battle, Constantine saw a cross in the heavens with the words "In this sign you will conquer." He used the cross as his battle standard and defeated his enemy.

Until the end of the sixth century, crosses were shown without the figure of the Redeemer. Today, the crucifix — a cross with the body of Jesus — usually represents Our Lord suffering.

The crucifix has been the inspiration and comfort of millions. When we pray before a crucifix, we call to mind that our Lord Jesus Christ suffered and died for us, and for our sins, and redeems us with his blood.

Behold, O good and sweetest Jesus, I cast myself upon my knees in your sight, and with the most fervent desire of my soul I pray and beseech you to impress upon my heart lively sentiments of faith, hope, and charity, true repentance for my sins, and a most firm purpose of amendment, while with deep affection and grief of soul I consider within myself and mentally contemplate your five most precious wounds, having before my eyes that which David, the prophet, long ago spoke in your own person concerning you, my Jesus: "They have pierced my hands and my feet; they have numbered all my bones."

16. The Nicene Creed (The Profession of Faith)

The Nicene Creed emphasizes the divinity, the divine nature, of Christ. This creed was introduced into the liturgy in the sixth century, and it is the creed, or statement of belief, that is included in our profession of faith at Mass today.

We believe in one God,
the Father, the Almighty,
maker of heaven and earth,
of all that is seen and unseen.

We believe in one Lord, Jesus Christ,
the only Son of God,

eternally begotten of the Father,
God from God, Light from Light,
true God from true God,
begotten, not made, one in Being with the
Father.
Through him all things were made.
For us men and for our salvation
he came down from heaven:
by the power of the Holy Spirit
he was born of the Virgin Mary, and
became man.
For our sake he was crucified under Pontius
Pilate;
he suffered, died, and was buried.
On the third day he rose again
in fulfillment of the Scriptures;
he ascended into heaven
and is seated at the right hand of the
Father.
He will come again in glory to judge the living
and the dead,
and his kingdom will have no end.

We believe in the Holy Spirit, the Lord, the
giver of life,
who proceeds from the Father and the Son.
With the Father and the Son he is worshiped
and glorified.
He has spoken through the prophets.

We believe in one holy catholic and apostolic
    Church.
We acknowledge one baptism for the
    forgiveness of sins.
We look for the resurrection of the dead,
    and the life of the world to come. Amen.

III.
PATRONS FOR PRISONERS

Although Our Lord, Our Lady, and all the saints are willing to help anyone, at any time, there are some saints, and some titles for Christ and His Blessed Mother, that traditionally have been favorites of prisoners worldwide. The Holy Child of Atocha (Santo Niño de Atocha) and the Just Judge (Justo Juez) are two names for Christ that many prisoners especially contemplate. Mary — under her titles of Our Lady of Atocha, Our Lady of Ransom, and Our Lady of Hope — is Mother to all, especially those incarcerated or held captive. Our Lady of Guadalupe also called herself our Mother.

May Our Lord and Our Lady bless you and lead you to the Light from Light, true God from true God, who loves you as his own child.

OUR LADY OF ATOCHA AND HER HOLY CHILD, SANTO NIÑO DE ATOCHA

Tradition says devotion to Our Lady of Atocha originated in Antioch, and that St. Luke the Evangelist was the artist who made the first Blessed Mother and Child image.

In Spain, during the dark years of the Moorish invaders, Catholics were persecuted for their faith. In Atocha, a suburb of Madrid, many of the Spanish men were thrown into Moorish

dungeons. The Moors did not feed their prisoners, so food had to be taken to the jail by the
families. At one time, the Moorish caliph or-
dered that no one except children twelve years
old and younger would be permitted to bring
the food. Those with young children would
manage to keep their relatives alive, but what of
the others?

The women of the town went to the parish
church, where there was a statue of Our Lady
of Atocha holding the baby Jesus. They begged
Our Lady to help them find a way to feed their
husbands, sons, and brothers. Soon the children
came home from the prison with a strange story.

Those prisoners who had no young children to feed them were being visited, and fed,
by a young boy. None of the children knew who
he was. But the little water gourd he carried
was never empty, and there was always plenty of
bread in his basket to feed all of the hapless prisoners who had no children to bring them their
food. He always came at night, slipping past the
sleeping guards, or smiling politely at those who
were alert.

Those who had asked Our Lady of Atocha
for a miracle began to suspect the identity of
the little boy. As if to confirm the miracle they
had prayed for, the shoes on the statue of the

child Jesus were worn down. When they replaced the shoes with new ones, these, too, were quickly worn out.

After the Moors were driven from Spain in 1492, the Spanish people continued to invoke the aid of Our Lady and her Holy Child. They especially asked help for those who were in jail and those who were "imprisoned" in the mines.

When the Spaniards came to the New World, they brought along the devotion to Our Lady and her miracle-working Holy Infant Pilgrim. In 1540, Spanish miners built a church in Plateros, Mexico, a tiny village near the mines of Fresnillo, and dedicated it in honor of El Niño de Santa Maria de Atocha. Here the Holy Child continued his miracles, working for those who appealed to him, through his mother, for help.

The original statue in the shrine, donated by a rich mine owner, was made as a duplicate of the one in Spain. The image of the Holy Child was removable, and it was often borrowed when a woman was about to give birth. At one time, the image of the Holy Child was lost, and its replacement was carved with dark, Indian features.

Today, the shrine is a major place of pilgrimage in Mexico. Through a century of revolution, Mexico has provided many prisoners for the Holy Child to aid. Annually, other miraculous cures and escapes are reported there.

The child Jesus wears a velvet suit with a wide lace collar and frilled cuffs. He has a broad hat with feathers. His shoes are buckled. In Mexico, the shoes are usually made of silver or gold. He carries a basket of bread and a staff from which hangs his water gourd. The cockleshell on his short cape comes from his Spanish origin; it is a Spanish symbol denoting that he is a pilgrim.

In the 1800s, a man from New Mexico made a pilgrimage to Fresnillo and took back with him a small statue of the Holy Child. This statue was enshrined in Chimayo, near Santa Fe. Here, the devotion grew, just as it had when it came to the New World.

Some of the first American troops to see action in World War II were from the New Mexico National Guard. Although they fought bravely on Corregidor, with its underground tunnels and defenses, the island eventually fell into enemy hands. The Catholics remembered that the Santo Niño de Atocha had long been considered a patron of all who were trapped or imprisoned. Many of them made a vow that if they survived the war, they would make a pilgrimage from Santa Fe to Chimayo in thanksgiving.

At the end of the war, two thousand pilgrims, veterans of Corregidor, the Bataan Death March, and Japanese prison camps, together with their families, walked the long and rough road from Santa Fe to Chimayo. Some walked barefoot to the little adobe shrine.

A Prayer to Santo Niño de Atocha

Beloved Santo Niño de Atocha, I beg you to free me from my self-made prison of sin. Deliver me from all the evil of the day. Holy Infant Pilgrim, take my hand and lead me on my pilgrimage through life to my heavenly home with you. Amen.

JUSTO JUEZ (JESUS, THE JUST JUDGE)

Jesus, the Just Judge, is a title of Christ much loved by those who have ever had contact with the legal system. It is a reminder that Christ will judge the living and the dead.

There is an image often seen in Mexico and other Spanish-speaking countries that is called *Justo Juez*, or "Just Judge." Jesus is invoked under this title when facing trials in daily living or when facing court battles. The picture symbolizes the Passion of Christ. Vividly, it calls to mind that through his death and resurrection, Christ is the one, true, and Just Judge of all mankind.

Jesus, crucified and crowned with thorns, is at the center of the picture. The artist has included many items of the Passion. The post from the scourging, the whip and flagellum, the ropes that bound Christ, the spear that pierced his side, the hammer, and other items are shown. A rooster and sun represent Peter's denial. Veronica's veil, showing the face of Christ, hangs on the pillar. Even the dice that the soldiers cast to divide Jesus' clothes are shown. A careful inspection of this picture can lead the viewer to contemplate the entire Passion of Our Lord. Prayers to Jesus under the title of the Just Judge call on him to obtain justice and mercy for the petitioner through the grace of his precious blood.

(Unfortunately, like many other true Catholic devotions, devotion to the Just Judge has been corrupted and transformed into an almost magical symbol in some places. Botanicas that market items for Santeria and for the spiritists sell "magical" candles and "lucky mojo charms" of Justo Juez, which are practically "guaranteed" to keep the owner safe from judicial prosecution; no mention is made as to whether the petitioner is guilty or not.)

In the true spirit of repentance and love, we call on Christ to judge us with justice and mercy.

A Prayer to the Just Judge

Jesus, you are the divine and Just Judge of all mankind. May your cross be my shield against all evil. Erase all sin and hatred from my heart. Through the merits of your precious blood, grant me peace. Amen.

OUR LADY OF RANSOM (OUR LADY OF MERCY)

Our Lady of Ransom (the feast day is September 24) is a Marian title that commemorates the beginning of the Mercedarian Order by St. Peter Nolasco in 1218. The name comes from the Spanish word *merced*, or "mercy."

As a young knight in Spain, Peter Nolasco gave his wealth to the Church and, after a vision of the Blessed Mother, began a work to ransom the Christian captives of the Moors. Today, the work of the Mercedarians centers on helping people escape their man-made prisons of sin and on reconciliation with God through Mary.

The pictures of Our Lady of Ransom often show Mary holding chains. These are symbolic of the chains of sin that she offers to remove from those who come to her in faith and love. As our Mother of Mercy, she offers us the redeeming love of her crucified Son and his divine mercy.

Throughout history, prisoners have appealed to Mary under her titles of Our Lady of Ransom and Our Lady of Mercy, to help them reconcile with God and gain peace in their hearts.

A Prayer to Our Lady of Mercy

O Mother of Mercy, help of Christians, I trust in your tender pity and beg you to hear my prayer. Obtain for me all the graces needed for my temporal and spiritual needs. Ransom me from the bonds of my sin; release the chains that hold me to the things of this world. Comfort my soul with peace, and fill my heart with love. In the name of your Son, Jesus Christ, I pray. Amen.

OUR LADY OF GUADALUPE

By Rev. Dennis Evenson

The story of the miraculous image of Our Lady of Guadalupe is 470 years old, but, unfortunately, still is not well known in North America. Yet, when these events took place in 1531, there was no Canada, no United States of America, and no United States of Mexico. The river now known as the Rio Grande was just a river, not a national boundary. It was all just America, when the geographic center of the

New World became the site of the first great evangelization in the Americas.

The Indian narrative is simple. Juan Diego, about fifty-seven years old, a humble peasant and recent convert to the Catholic faith, is on his way to Saturday Mass, "very early in the morning," and to catechism lessons. It is December 9, 1531, at that time the feast of the Immaculate Conception. Lovely music attracts his attention when he is at the foot of the rocky and barren hill of Tepeyac. A woman's voice affectionately calls to him by name: "Juanito, Juan Dieguito." The music stops.

The Lady tells him she is the "ever Virgin Mary, Mother of the true God." Then she tells him where she wants a church built for the people, where "I will hear their weeping, their complaints, and heal all their sorrows, hardships, and sufferings." Juan Diego is to be her messenger to the recently arrived bishop-elect from Spain, Juan de Zumárraga, a holy and zealous Franciscan friar who truly wanted to help the Indians. The new bishop has much confidence and trust in the Blessed Virgin Mary and her unfailing help, and has entrusted New Spain (the name for the Spanish territories in and around present-day Mexico) to her.

Juan Diego sets out for the bishop's house. The bishop's staff is suspicious of this poor Indian. After much delay, he is let in to see the bishop, who, however, fears the story is just a dream on the part of this new convert. He refuses the request for a new church, and Juan is saddened by this. Mary then appears a second time to Juan Diego, to encourage him to go see the bishop again.

After more difficulties, he is able to see the bishop once more. This time the bishop asks for some special sign to prove the truth of Juan's story. For a third time, the Lady appears, encouraging Juan anew. She promises to give him the sign for the bishop the next day. But on that day, Juan must look for a doctor to treat his very sick uncle, Juan Bernardino, also a recent convert. So Juan Diego does not keep his appointment with the Lady.

But the doctor's efforts do not help Juan's uncle. And so, very early the next day, Juan Diego leaves to call a priest for his dying uncle. Juan even tries to avoid running into the Lady by taking another route. She finds him anyway, and in this fourth apparition she assures him he must have no fear for his uncle's health, for she is the merciful Mother of all. "Am I not here, I who am your Mother?" she asks. "Are you not under my care? Do I not hold you as a dear child in the folds of my garments? Am I not your hope and salvation? Is there anything more you need?"

She now directs Juan to go to the top of the barren hill where he first met her. There, she tells him, he will find fresh roses, laden with dewdrops like glistening pearls, to gather into his tilma, or cloak, to bring to her to arrange. Roses are out of season in December, and nothing else is growing at the top of the hill now either, so Juan thinks this surely will be the sign for the bishop.

Unbeknown to Juan, the bishop secretly has been hoping to see once again his beloved Castilian roses. As the Lady has instructed him to do, Juan gathers the roses and joyfully leaves for the bishop's residence, with the roses rearranged by the Lady.

Again, after more delays and difficulties, Juan is allowed to see the bishop. He gives the Lady's message to him and tells the bishop he now has the sign that the bishop requested. With that, he unfolds his tilma, and the roses spill out onto the floor. The bishop falls to his knees, praying with tear-filled eyes. The others in the room likewise fall to their knees. Juan himself is bewildered. He then sees there on the tilma, amazingly, and in gloriously magnificent tones, the image of Mary exactly as she had appeared to him on the hill at Tepeyac. Certainly, this is the reason the Lady herself rearranged the roses to present to the bishop.

Now Juan is immediately treated with respect and deference by the bishop's staff. The bishop and all present process with the image to his chapel, to enthrone the image there, until a more suitable church can be built. Within two weeks, a chapel is built for the image, and Mary's image is moved there from the bishop's chapel, for the veneration of all.

Juan returns home to find his uncle cured. The uncle tells him the Lady had likewise appeared to him, and cured him, shortly after Juan left for a priest. She also gave the uncle her name: "Holy Mary, ever Virgin of Guadalupe." The name Guadalupe means "She who crushes the stone serpent." The reign of the false gods was over.

To the end of his life, at age seventy-four, in 1548, Juan Diego was the guardian of the tilma, telling the story over and over again of the merciful Mother who wished to lead all peoples to her divine Son.

Under her title of Our Lady of Guadalupe, Mary is also invoked as Health of the Sick. In the image, Mary is depicted as a young mestiza maiden, one who is of both Native American and

European background. Thus, she is known as La Morenita, or "The Little Brown One." She is pictured as a pregnant woman, about age fifteen, holy and dignified. The image is also recognized as a version of the Immaculate Conception.

Such is the simple tradition. The fame of the miracle spread rapidly. To this day, the story of the miraculous image of Our Lady of Guadalupe attracts and inspires. Certainly, the greatest miracle of all is the effect Our Lady of Guadalupe has had in bringing people to the true faith and worship of the true God.

Blood had flowed for centuries in the Aztec Empire from human sacrifice to false gods by the time Hernando Cortes landed on the Mexican coast in 1519. By 1521, that empire had fallen. Ten years later, the Indian people were on the verge of revolt. The Mother of the true God then entered the scene in a unique way in 1531. She reconciled and united peoples and cultures that had been at violent odds with each other.

Attempts before 1531 by the Spanish missionaries to teach the Catholic faith brought very few and slow results. But through this miraculous image, the Indians came to understand the teaching and preaching of the missionaries, for they now understood these teachings through their own outlook and culture. The Catholic faith took hold, as the image of Mary was imprinted, not only on Juan Diego's cloak, but also on the hearts of the people.

Mary of Guadalupe, in this way, became the greatest evangelizer of all time. No one else has ever brought so many millions to the Catholic faith in so short a time. Her presence alone, without any violence, was enough to end the human sacrifice so prevalent at the time. For this reason, Mary of Guadalupe is now regularly invoked as patroness of all pro-life efforts to end the human sacrifice brought about by abortion.

At Guadalupe, Mary came among us as our Mother. We are to respond to her as children of the same Mother. In moments of difficulty and joy, we come before this Lady, our Mother, who loves us all without exception, without regard to the color of our skin or our national borders.

She came in 1531 to redirect the efforts of the Spanish conquerors, who sought the physical conquest of land and people. Mary would achieve the conquest of hearts for her divine Son. Her coming in this way meant the birth of a new civilization and culture, and of a new Church in the New World that would see far beyond individual races and physical conquest.

Various scientific studies have been done on the tilma, and modern science continues to reveal much about the picture. Neither natural nor animal nor mineral coloring is found on it. There were no synthetic colors in 1531. Scientists over the years have shown it is impossible to paint such an image on a fabric of this fiber. The *ayate* fiber used by the Indians for such a cloak lasts only about twenty years. Studies with infrared rays reveal no traces of paint and no treatment of the fabric in any way. So the picture remains humanly inexplicable, a miracle.

Even the eyes of Mary on this image have been studied. Enlargement of the pupils of her eyes shows various images, up to thirteen people, including Juan Diego and the bishop. We can be sure that we, too, spiritually speaking, are ever in the pupils of the eyes of Mary, Mother of the true God.

Popes through the ages have acclaimed this image and what it should mean for us. In 1754, upon being presented with a copy of the original and hearing its story, Pope Benedict XIV exclaimed, in the words of the psalmist: "[He] has not done this for other nations" (Ps 147:20).

Pope Leo XIII authorized the first crowning of the image, which took place on October 12, 1895. In 1945, on the golden anniversary of that event, Pope Pius XII named Our Lady of Guadalupe "Empress of the Americas"— North,

Central, and South. In a radio address to Mexico City at that time, he said: "We are certain that as long as you are recognized as Queen and Mother, America and Mexico will be saved." He also declared that the image had been painted "by brushes that were not of this world."

Blessed Pope John XXIII called Our Lady of Guadalupe the "Mother and Teacher of the faith to the peoples of the Americas." Pope Paul VI honored the image with the rare gift of a golden rose.

Pope John Paul II's first visit outside Italy as pontiff was to the Dominican Republic and Mexico in 1979, and to Our Lady's shrine in Mexico City. As any other pilgrim, he came to lay his prayers and petitions at the feet of Our Lady of Guadalupe. He returned to Mexico on May 6, 1990, to beatify Juan Diego. In this way, the Holy Father indicated the true existence of Juan Diego and the importance of Our Lady of Guadalupe and her message. Juan Diego was called by Mary to be a lay apostle who would help stop evil and help spread truth and understanding.

A Prayer to Our Lady of Guadalupe

O Virgin of Guadalupe, Holy Mother of God, carry me close to Our Lord under your Immaculate

Heart. Hear my weeping and complaints, heal my sorrows, hardships, and sufferings. Let me change my life and, like Blessed Juan Diego, let me help stop evil in this world and help spread truth and understanding. Through Christ, Our Lord, I pray. Amen.

OUR LADY OF HOPE

At the conclusion of the Second Vatican Council's Dogmatic Constitution on the Church, this is said about Mary: "Just as the Mother of Jesus, glorified in body and soul in heaven, is the image and beginning of the Church as it is to be perfected in the world to come, so too does she shine forth on earth, until the day of the Lord shall come, as a sign of sure hope and solace to the people of God during its sojourn on earth" (no. 68).

The council fathers then added: "The entire body of the faithful pours forth instant supplications to the Mother of God and Mother of men that she, who aided the beginnings of the Church by her prayers, may now, exalted as she is above all the angels and saints, intercede before her Son in the fellowship of all the saints, until all families of people, whether they are honored with the title of Christian or whether they still do not know the Savior, may be happily gathered together in peace and harmony into one people of God, for the glory of the Most Holy and Undivided Trinity" (no. 69).

It is because of Mary's loving concern for us that we can say with confidence that the Mother

of God and Mother of men truly is Our Lady
of Hope.

Litany of Our Lady of Hope

By Most Reverend Robert J. Baker

Mary, you bring us life,	**hear our prayer.**
Mary, you bring us peace,	**hear our prayer.**
Mary, you bring us hope,	**hear our prayer.**
Mary, you bring us Christ, the Son of the Living God,	**hear our prayer.**
Mother of the Forgiving Christ,	**intercede for us.**
Mother of the Reconciling Christ,	**intercede for us.**
Mother of the Redeeming Christ,	**intercede for us.**
Mother of the Victorious Christ,	**intercede for us.**
Mother of the Sick,	**pray for us.**
Mother of the Suffering,	**pray for us.**
Mother of the Sinful,	**pray for us.**
Mother of the Sorrowful,	**pray for us.**
Mother of the Distressed,	**pray for us.**
Mother of the Bereaved,	**pray for us.**
Mother of the Widowed,	**pray for us.**
Mother of the Married and Single,	**pray for us.**

Mother of Those Who Struggle in
    Marriage or are Separated,   **pray for us.**
Mother of the Parentless,   **pray for us.**
Mother of the Childless,   **pray for us.**
Mother of the Lonely,   **pray for us.**
Mother of the Neglected,   **pray for us.**
Mother of the Abused,   **pray for us.**
Mother of the Abandoned,   **pray for us.**
Mother of the Unborn,   **pray for us.**
Mother of the Parenting Unwed,   **pray for us.**
Mother of the Homebound,   **pray for us.**
Mother of the Hospitalized,   **pray for us.**
Mother of the Institutionalized,   **pray for us.**
Mother of the Imprisoned,   **pray for us.**
Mother of Those on Death Row,   **pray for us.**
Mother of Those Who Hunger
    and Thirst,   **pray for us.**
Mother of All the Impoverished,   **pray for us.**
Mother of the Afflicted,   **pray for us.**
Mother of the Homeless,   **pray for us.**
Mother of the Helpless,   **pray for us.**
Mother of the Hopeless,   **pray for us.**
Mother of the Addicted,   **pray for us.**
Mother of Wandering Youth,   **pray for us.**
Mother of the Frail Elderly,   **pray for us.**
Mother of the Unchurched,   **pray for us.**
Mother of Unbelievers,   **pray for us.**

Mother of Those Facing Financial
   Failure,   **pray for us.**
Mother of Those Facing Uncertain
   Futures,   **pray for us.**
Mother of Nations in Turmoil and
   Under Siege,   **pray for us.**
Mother of Migrants and Immigrants,   **pray for us.**
Mother of the Victims of Crime,   **pray for us.**
Mother of the Victims of War,   **pray for us.**
Mother of the Victims of Famine,   **pray for us.**
Mother of the Victims of all Natural
   Disasters,   **pray for us.**
Mother of Those Who Suffer Defeats,   **pray for us.**
Mother of Those Who Win Hollow
   Victories,   **pray for us.**
Mother of the Disabled,   **pray for us.**
Mother of the Emotionally Distraught,   **pray for us.**
Mother of the Despairing,   **pray for us.**
Mother of the Dying,   **pray for us.**
Mother of Those Who Mourn,   **pray for us.**
Mother of Those Who Call Upon You,   **pray for us.**
Mother of Those Who Trust in You,   **pray for us.**

Mary, you bring us life,   **hear our prayer.**
Mary, you bring us peace,   **hear our prayer.**
Mary, you bring us hope,   **hear our prayer.**

Mary, you bring us Christ,
   the Son of the Living God,
   who has conquered
   all the forces of evil,   **hear our prayer.**

Christ, hear us,   **Christ graciously hear us.**
Lord Jesus, hear our
   prayer,   **Lord Jesus, hear our prayer.**

Let us pray:

Lord Jesus, we pray to you for the gift of hope and
the grace of perseverance through the prayer and
intercession of the Blessed Virgin Mary, your
mother and your gift as Mother to all of us, the
hope of all who are in distress. May she always
lead us closer to you, her Son, Jesus Christ, Our
Lord. Amen.

IV.
PATRON SAINTS FOR
PRISONERS

A number of saints, both from ancient times and from our own age, particularly appeal to those in jail.

What is a saint? A saint is a real person, just like us, who has lived with holiness of life and heroic virtue, and who is proclaimed by the Church to be fit to serve as a spiritual model and able to intercede for us in the presence of God. Saints were not "angels" on earth. Some of them were great sinners before they decided to give their lives to God. They all struggled with faults and failures, weaknesses and sins, just as we do.

Saints come in different colors — all the beautiful colors of the human rainbow. There are saints from every part of the world. Some were young, some old. Some saints were martyrs. Martyrs are people who were killed while defending the faith; they chose to shed their blood for the love of God rather than deny him.

All the saints chose to make God their greatest love, and to accept the great love he stands willing to give us.

ADELAIDE

Feast day: December 16

Born in 931, St. Adelaide was a princess of Burgundy. When she refused to marry the son of the marquis of Ivres, he had her imprisoned in a castle. A priest named Martin discovered where she was and dug an underground tunnel to rescue her. She later married the emperor Otto and was known for her charitable works. She worked hard to convert the Slavic peoples. She died in 999.

CHARLES OF BLOIS

Feast day: September 29

Blessed Charles, born in 1320, was a duke of Brittany. In 1346, he was defeated in battle, deported to England, and imprisoned. Although a ransom was paid, he was kept in prison for nine years before he was allowed to return home to France. He remained a devout Catholic and was faithful in prayer. After his death in 1364, many miracles were reported at his tomb.

COSMOS AND DAMIEN

Feast day: September 26

Sts. Cosmos and Damian were twin brothers, born in Arabia in the third century. They became physicians and went to Syria to practice the art of healing, curing the sicknesses of the soul as well as of the body. They took no payment for their services and brought many to the Christian faith. When the Roman emperor

Diocletian began persecuting the Christians, the brothers were arrested, tortured, and beheaded.

DISMAS, THE GOOD THIEF

Feast day: March 25

St. Dismas is known as the "Good Thief," who was crucified with Christ on Calvary. The other thief is known as Gestas. There is an old legend that the two thieves held up the Holy Family on their way to Egypt. Seeing the young baby, Dismas convinced Gestas not to molest them. The baby Jesus predicted that both thieves would be crucified with him in Jerusalem, and that Dismas would accompany him to heaven. We do know from the Bible (see Lk 23:39-43) that while hanging on his cross, Dismas repented of his sins and Our Lord promised to take him to paradise.

HUBERT

Feast day: November 3

St. Hubert was the son of a duke, and as a charming young man he pursued worldly comforts and pleasures. His favorite hobby was hunting. One Good Friday morning, when the faithful were at church, Hubert chose instead to go on the chase. As he followed a magnificent stag, the deer turned and Hubert was astounded to see a crucifix between its antlers. A voice spoke to him and said, "Hubert, unless you turn to the Lord and lead a holy life, you will quickly go to hell." He converted immediately and gave all his wealth to the poor. Prisoners were especially dear to him, and he carried food to them secretly, passing it through the windows of their dungeons. He died in 727.

JOSEPH CAFASSO

Feast day: June 23

St. Joseph Cafasso was an Italian priest born in 1811. He was known for his work with prisoners and convicts. He could not bear the thought of an unrepentant soul being condemned to hell, so with patience and love he did all in his power to show the prisoners the love and mercy of God. He accompanied more than sixty men on their way to be hanged, and each of them died converted to the faith. Joseph lovingly called those men his "hanging saints." He died in 1860.

LEONARD

Feast day: November 6

Little is known about the life of this sixth-century saint, but according to legend he belonged to a noble French family during the reign of King Clovis. He obtained from the king the release of a great number of prisoners. In the twelfth century, along the highways of France there were many manacles and chains hanging on stone crosses. These were put there by former prisoners in thanksgiving to St. Leonard. They believed the saint's assistance had helped in their release from jail.

LOUIS IX

Feast day: August 25

St. Louis, born in 1214, was the king of France. During one crusade, Louis was taken prisoner by the Saracens. Eventually, a ransom was paid and he was set free. He went to the Holy Land for a while before he returned to France. He was known for protecting the common people from abuse, enacting fair laws, and serving as a mediator among other nations. He died in 1270 while setting out on another crusade. He is a patron saint of the Secular Franciscan Order.

NICHOLAS

Feast day: December 6

St. Nicholas is one of the most popular saints of all times. Although almost nothing factual is

known of his life, except that he was the bishop
of Myra in the fourth century, legends about his
life and miracles abound. Twice Nicholas came
to the rescue of three innocent men who were
unjustly accused and condemned to death. He
went to the prison, forced the guards to release
the prisoners, and then confronted the governor who had been bribed to accuse the men.
The governor acknowledged his wrongdoing in
the presence of three officers. Later, these three
officers also were accused and condemned, but
Nicholas miraculously freed them.

PETER THE APOSTLE

Feast day: June 29

St. Peter was the leader of the apostles, the
first pope, and is known as the custodian of the
"keys to the kingdom of heaven" (Mt 16:19).
Simon Peter was a fisherman when Christ called
him to become an apostle. The name Peter means
"Rock," for Christ told Peter that he was the
rock on which Christ would build his Church.
When Jesus was arrested, Peter at first tried to
defend him, cutting off the ear of one of those
who was attempting to arrest Our Lord. Later,
just as Jesus had predicted, Peter denied he even
knew Jesus. After the Crucifixion, Peter was sorry

for denying Christ and wept bitterly. The risen Christ appeared to him and told him to "feed my lambs" (Jn 21:15). Peter began his work of building up the early Church. He was thrown into prison about the year 43 by King Herod Agrippa, but an angel miraculously helped him to escape, breaking his chains and opening the door of the prison. He continued his work until he was captured and martyred by the emperor Nero, probably in the year 64. Tradition says that he was crucified upside down, as he felt unworthy to die in the same manner as Our Lord. Because of his miraculous escape from prison, he has long been a favorite patron of prisoners.

In addition to the above traditional patrons, the following two saints, a blessed, and a saint-to-be from our own times are particular favorites of many prisoners. Their advice and their lives can give hope and joy to those who suffer in today's prisons.

JOHN BOSCO

Feast day: January 31

St. John Bosco particularly is considered a patron for youthful offenders. He was born in Becchi, Italy, in 1815 and was ordained a priest at the age of twenty-five. Later that year, he went to Turin to continue his studies under Father Joseph Cafasso (see page 120).

Father Cafasso was the chaplain for the city's prisons, and he invited Don Bosco (as he came to be known) to accompany him to visit his beloved prisoners. Don Bosco was reluctant to go. He was upset at the thought of the wretched conditions in the prisons. The prisons were damp, unhealthy, and crowded; the prisoners were guilty of all forms of horrible crimes. Then Don Bosco remembered Jesus' words: "I was . . . in prison and you visited me" (Mt 25:35–36).

Father Cafasso was much loved by the prisoners, and he taught his young associate well, so from the very first Don Bosco was able to inspire the prisoners to trust in God's mercy. In particular, it was the plight of the poor youths in prison that touched Don Bosco's great heart. Many youths, guilty of only minor offenses, were thrown into the stinking jails along with the hardened criminals. There were many orphans in Turin at this time, and sometimes boys as young as seven or eight were imprisoned for stealing food.

Don Bosco became more convinced that when these youths were treated with great love, even the roughest and most rebellious would yield to change. He helped many of the boys discover mercy and pardon in the very place where they had been condemned to be punished. He founded a religious order to care for these street children. Later, he helped St. Mary Mazzarello begin the same type of work for girls.

Don Bosco was always thoughtful and courteous to the guards and the executioners, and they began to aid him in his undertakings for the prisoners' physical and spiritual welfare. With their goodwill, he continued his prison ministry for thirty years, even after anti-clerical officials issued harassing orders to restrict his visits. When someone's term was up, Don Bosco was there to help him reenter society and make an honest living.

Eventually, Father Cafasso told Don Bosco that his most important work would be to care for the abandoned youths of the city in order to prevent their falling into situations that would lead to their imprisonment. The sight of so many young lives being wasted in prison was a compelling motive for Don Bosco's work. He based his "preventative system" on a joyful, loving kindness that showed the young that they were loved, and this system helped them train for gainful occupations.

Don Bosco died in 1888, but the Salesian Order carries on his work throughout the world today.

MAXIMILIAN KOLBE

Feast day: August 14

St. Maximilian particularly is considered a patron of political prisoners.

Raymond Kolbe was born in 1894 in Poland, the second son of pious weavers. A bright child, he was also mischievous. One day his exasperated mother threw up her hands and cried out, "What is to become of you?"

The little prankster soon began to spend a great deal of time in front of the family altar, with its lovely image of Our Lady. Later, he confessed to his mother, "I asked the Blessed Virgin what would become of me. Then she appeared to me holding two crowns; one was white, representing purity, and the other was red, for martyrdom. Our Lady asked me which I would choose. I answered, 'I choose them both!' " The lady smiled and disappeared.

In 1907, Raymond entered the Order of Friars Minor Conventual (Franciscans), taking the name Maximilian as his religious name. He was a good student. While studying at the

Gregorian University in Rome, he organized a group he called the Militia of the Immaculate. The group, dedicated to Our Lady, worked for conversions to the Church. He was ordained in 1918, returned to Poland, and devoted much of his time to spreading the Militia.

Father Kolbe understood the value of the mass media as a tool for spreading the Good News, and began to produce a newsletter and other publications. In 1929, he founded a friary devoted to this work. Later, he went to Japan to establish the work of the Militia there. He returned to Poland in 1936. By that time, the friary was publishing magazines with a total circulation of more than a million copies and a daily paper with a circulation of more than 125,000.

The German Army invaded Poland in September 1939, and Father Kolbe was arrested, but later released. The friars set up a machine-repair shop for farming equipment and assisted about five thousand Jewish refugees. In 1940, Father Kolbe began publishing his newsletter again. He was arrested again, in 1941, and sent to prison in Auschwitz.

Everything in that hell on earth was designed to destroy an inmate's humanity. The personnel of the death camp did their best to grind down and degrade all the prisoners, but the sturdy priest retained his Franciscan joy and inspired the other prisoners.

One night, a few months later, a prisoner escaped. The commandant called out the prisoners, lined them up, and demanded the death of ten prisoners, as punishment for the escape. As he pointed out ten prisoners to die, one of them cried out, "What will happen to my wife and children?" Father Kolbe stepped forward and challenged the officer: "I have no family. Let me take his place." His request was granted.

The ten were put in starvation bunkers. Witnesses testified that Father Kolbe continued to encourage the starving men, constantly praying, singing, and reciting the Rosary. After two weeks, his agony was ended by a lethal injection.

St. Maximilian reminds us, "The real conflict is inner conflict. Beyond armies of occupation and the catacombs of concentration camps, there are two irreconcilable enemies in the depth of every soul: good and evil, sin and love. And what use are victories on the battlefield if we ourselves are defeated in our innermost personal selves?"

MIGUEL PRO

Feast day: November 23

Blessed Miguel Pro, S.J., was executed during the persecution of the Catholic Church in Mexico. The photographs of his execution were widely distributed, and graphically illustrated the plight of Catholic Mexico to a shocked world. Father Pro was beatified as a martyr, but it is his heart, in addition to his blood, that marks his holiness.

Born in 1891, in Guadalupe, in the Mexican state of Zacatecas, Miguel was the oldest son of a large and loving mining family. From early childhood, he lived life with happy enthusiasm and with an obvious inclination for tricks and jokes. But the working man, the poor, and the disenfranchised were the special objects of his charity. At his ordination, he prayed to be useful to souls, recognizing that "to do them good, one must love them passionately." That love grew daily in his soul and flowered in the greatest proof: the sacrifice of his life.

Known everywhere for his high spirits and happiness, he teasingly referred to himself as the apostle "whom drunkards hobnobbed with, whom vendors winked at, whom the flower and cream of rascality took to their hearts." In his clandestine ministry, Father Pro met many souls bearing heavy crosses. He studied each one individually. "God alone," he said, "is the Master of souls."

Disclosing the secret of his love, Father Pro held a picture of the Heart of Jesus and exclaimed, "The cross of our Lord Jesus Christ! Let us study this precious book. . . . When our souls approach the Heart of Jesus, our love can neither fail nor fade. . . . When a heart has once drawn its sap from the wood of the cross, it can no longer turn away. I know this by experience."

Perhaps Father Pro understood the suffering of others so well because he, too, had suffered. In spite of his deepest affliction, however, he always kept his cheerful, exuberant nature. As a novice, he was expelled, along with the Jesuits, from his beloved homeland. One could always tell when the news from Mexico was bad because he would go out of his way at those times to play his most outrageous tricks to cheer his fellow exiles, hiding his own sorrow under a mask of high spirits.

Father Pro concealed ever-increasing stomach problems by telling a joke whenever the pain came, giving himself an excuse to hold his sides and make funny faces to cover a grimace of agony. But, far from home, he was grief-stricken to receive the news of his mother's death.

In 1926, Father Pro was allowed to return to Mexico. It is unlikely his superiors realized the extent of the danger there. Or perhaps they didn't believe he would live long, due to his poor health, and wanted to allow him to die at home.

Within days of his arrival, the churches were closed, and Father Pro began a hidden ministry. A natural actor, Father Pro used numerous disguises to go about his work, celebrating the sacraments and distributing temporal aid to the poor. His life reads like a spy novel: full of intrigue, full of danger. He was captured and jailed numerous times but managed to get himself released.

In his precarious situation, Father Pro understood the message of the cross. He wrote, "Does our life become from day to day more painful, more oppressive, more replete with sufferings? Blessed be [God] a thousand times who desires it so. If life be harder, love makes it also stronger, and only this love, grounded on suffering, can carry the cross of my Lord, Jesus Christ."

In November 1927, Father Pro's earthly ministry came to an end. He was betrayed, arrested, imprisoned — and without any trial, the order for his execution was given.

As Father Pro was led out, he blessed and forgave the firing squad. Refusing the traditional blindfold, he knelt in front of the bullet-riddled walls. Rosary in hand, his last request was for a moment of prayer. The order to fire was given. Through the explosion of the volley, his last words, strongly spoken, were heard: "*Viva Cristo Rey!*" ("Long live Christ the King").

JACQUES FESCH

Jacques Fesch, a young Frenchman, was a convicted murderer who was guillotined for his crime on September 30, 1957, at the age of twenty-seven. He has left us a testimony that can bring hope to even the most hardened of sinners. He was successfully able to resist the terrible temptation of despair and present a clear witness to the unconquerable strength of a God who is Love and whose love no crime can overpower.

The morning of his execution, Jacques awoke at three o'clock and told his guard that he had to "get ready at once." He was reading his prayer book peacefully when the prison chaplain arrived at five-thirty. He made his final confession and received, movingly, Communion. As they bound Jacques's hands, he remained peaceful and serene. He refused the traditional glass of rum and cigarette offered to the condemned at the moment of execution, but as he mounted the scaffold he asked the chaplain for the crucifix and kissed it fervently. Moments later, the blade of the guillotine fell.

Afterward, the chaplain said that Jacques had offered his life for his father, for those whom he loved, and for his victim. There was not the slightest note of rancor or bitterness.

Jacques Fesch entered prison an atheist. The first time the prison chaplain visited him, he sent the priest away, telling him that he had no faith. In the nearly four years he spent in prison, he returned to the Catholic faith and became a true contemplative. In addition, he was given a number of mystical insights and went to his execution in a spirit of faith and joy.

Some people may think that Jacques's conversion was a normal reaction. Imprisoned, stripped of everything, who else can you turn to but God? That is a simplistic view. It is not easy to allow yourself to be drawn from darkness to the point of emptying yourself of your own ego, whether in prison or in the world.

Over a period of time, a great interior transformation took place in the soul of Jacques Fesch. "And then, at the end of my first year in prison, a powerful wave of emotion swept over me, causing deep and brutal suffering. Within the space of a few hours, I came into possession of faith, with absolute certainty. I believed, and could no longer understand how I had ever not believed. Grace had come to me. A great joy flooded my soul and, above all, a deep peace."

Jacques Fesch was born April 6, 1930, the son of Belgian parents. His father was a bank president, an autocratic man and an atheist who made family life unbearable. His mother was loving but ineffectual. Jacques attended school for ten years, but the problems of his family had damaged his sense of security and his enthusiasm, and he did poorly in school. He quit school and worked at his father's bank until he left for military service. Later, his parents separated.

Jacques was tall and slender, with nice features. But his silence and timidity came across to many as apathy. He married Pierette Polack, a young girl from his hometown, and fathered a daughter, Veronica. Later, he wrote with brutal honesty: "I was a disturbed, unbalanced, and deeply unhappy person. I married because, in the first place, my wife was pregnant, and then too because I had found a semblance of warmth in my new family. . . . I did not love my wife, but we got along well and peaceably. My child I did love. But what is a child when one is twenty and has no moral stability?"

Later, in prison, he apparently grew to love Pierette. In his letters, he apologized to her, and he maintained a continued love and concern for his daughter.

After his military service, Jacques worked in a factory. The young couple, both immature, separated in October 1953. He borrowed money from his mother to start a business, but he blew it on a car instead. He became discouraged and longed for an easy solution.

The thought of escape from his miserable life became an obsession, and he made plans, with two other young men as accomplices, to rob a moneychanger. Before the planned attack, Jacques went to his father's home and stole a loaded revolver and a hammer.

One day in late February 1954, Jacques went to a moneychanger's shop, left, and then returned in the evening. He struck the old man there with the butt of the gun. Although the old man's head was bloodied, he managed to cry out for help, and the gun discharged a bullet that wounded Jacques's own hand.

Streaming blood, Jacques ran, but the blood caused him to be noticed. After hiding briefly in a building, he attempted to leave when he was recognized. A policeman shouted for him to put his hands up. Instead, seized with panic, he drew the revolver and fired a single shot that hit the policeman in the heart, killing him. Frantic to escape, he wounded a second man who attempted to capture him. He fired twice at two other pursuers, missing both, but was finally caught at a nearby subway station.

Upon his arrest, Jacques was subjected to the usual police interrogation and taken afterward to the Prison de la Sant in Paris. To her credit, Pierette stood by Jacques until his death. She forgave him and married him in a religious ceremony only a few days before his execution.

In writing of his crime to the prison chaplain, Jacques did not make excuses and never claimed that he was not guilty of the crime with which he had been charged. He explained that he was also guilty of other sins than the robbery and murder. He felt he would also have to answer for the pain he had caused his wife, his child, and others.

Jacques never studied theology; his theology came from the inner workings of God in his soul. He realized that his conversion was a gradual, progressive thing, but he moved from atheism to a marked, sincere faith.

"Before that, the true God was an indifferent tradition as far as I was concerned," Jacques
wrote in prison. "Now, he is all that matters. . . .
Then comes the struggle — silent, tragic —
between what I was and what I have become.
For the new creature who has been planted
within me calls for a response which I am free
to refuse. . . . I am amazed and surprised at the
change which grace has effected in me. . . . In
this radical experience which is overturning my
life and marking it indelibly, I perceive an on-
going need for spiritual renewal. . . . But God is
here. In him I have the strength to see and do
whatever I must, so as to be conformed to his
image. He unites my prayer to his will. The vo-
cation he gives me arouses a prayer within me,
which I address to him."

Appeals failed, and Jacques accepted his death
and offered it for those "whom the Lord wants
to save." He begged his family to prepare them-
selves in prayer, offering their grief to God, so
he might go in peace. Above all, he cautioned
them not to see divine injustice in his execution and told them, "God is not an automatic
distributor of temporal benefits to sinners who
have come upon hard times. He loves men and
has only one object: to give himself to them for
all eternity, not to give them a pleasant life on

earth which will generate sins, and then bring souls who have injured him to paradise!"

Realizing that love continues to exist, Jacques promised, "If God permits it, I will pray for all of you from heaven. There is a communion of souls, but for that we must be in the necessary state."

The Pope Speaks to Prisoners

When Pope John Paul II visited the prisoners of Rome's Regina Coeli Prison on July 9, 2000, his visit was symbolic of his wish to visit all of the prisoners in the world, to address all the places in the world where men and women are in prison. He said, "I come to tell you that God loves you and wants you to follow a path of rehabilitation and forgiveness, of truth and justice."

The pope pointed out that any man may be, in a certain sense, a prisoner. He declared, "Sin is the prison of the spirit." He explained, "Our sin has disrupted God's plan, and its effects are not only felt in human life but also in creation itself. . . . Sin is devastating. It drives peace from hearts and causes a chain of sufferings in human relationships."

The Holy Father spoke words of hope and peace, saying, "This is precisely the slavery from which the Spirit of God comes to deliver us. . . ."

"Therefore," he continued, "the Holy Spirit must pervade this prison where we are meeting and all the prisons of the world. Christ, the Son of God, became a prisoner; he let them tie his hands and then nail them to the cross precisely so that his Spirit could touch the heart of every man."

Later, in one of his talks, John Paul II shared the joy that the visit to the prisoners gave him. "Looking into their eyes, I tried to glimpse the sufferings, anxieties, and hopes of each one," he said. "I knew that in them I was meeting Christ, who identified with them in the Gospel to the point of saying: 'I was in prison and you came to me'" (Mt 25:36).

My Prayers

My Prayers

My Prayers

Our Sunday Visitor . . .
Your Source for Discovering
the Riches of the Catholic Faith

Our Sunday Visitor has an extensive line of materials for young children, teens, and adults. Our books, Bibles, booklets, CD-ROMs, audios, and videos are available in bookstores world-wide.

To receive a FREE full-line catalog or for more information, call **Our Sunday Visitor** at **1-800-348-2440**. Or write, **Our Sunday Visitor** / 200 Noll Plaza / Huntington, IN 46750.

- -

Our Sunday Visitor
200 Noll Plaza
Huntington, IN 46750
Toll free: **1-800-348-2440**
E-mail: osvbooks@osv.com
Website: www.osv.com